A KICK IN THE BELLY

A KICK IN THE BELLY

Women, Slavery and Resistance

Stella Dadzie

VERSO

London • New York

First published by Verso 2020
© Stella Dadzie 2020

1 3 5 7 9 10 8 6 4 2

Verso
UK: 6 Meard Street, London W1F 0EG
US: 20 Jay Street, Suite 1010, Brooklyn, NY 11201
versobooks.com

Verso is the imprint of New Left Books

ISBN-13: 978-1-78873-884-2
ISBN-13: 978-1-78873-885-9 (UK EBK)
ISBN-13: 978-1-78873-886-6 (US EBK)

British Library Cataloguing in Publication Data
A catalogue record for this book is available from the British Library

Library of Congress Cataloging-in-Publication Data
A catalog record for this book is available from the Library of Congress

Typeset in Garamond by Biblichor Ltd, Edinburgh
Printed and bound by CPI Group (UK) Ltd, Croydon CR0 4YY

For Olive Morris and Sylvia Erike.
Because your spirit lives on.

Contents

Overview of the Transatlantic Slave Trade, 1501–1867

Source: Yale University Press, © 2010

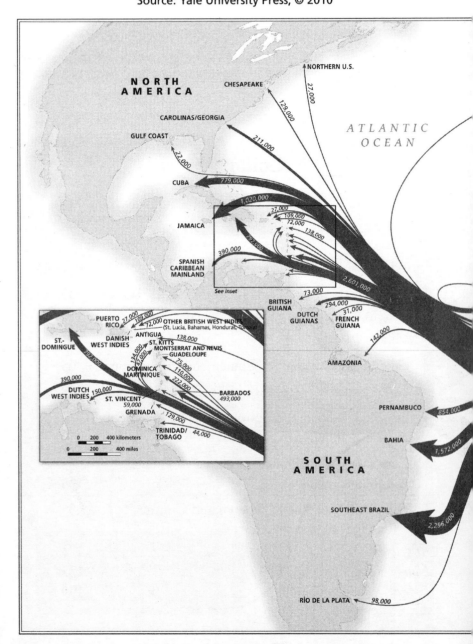

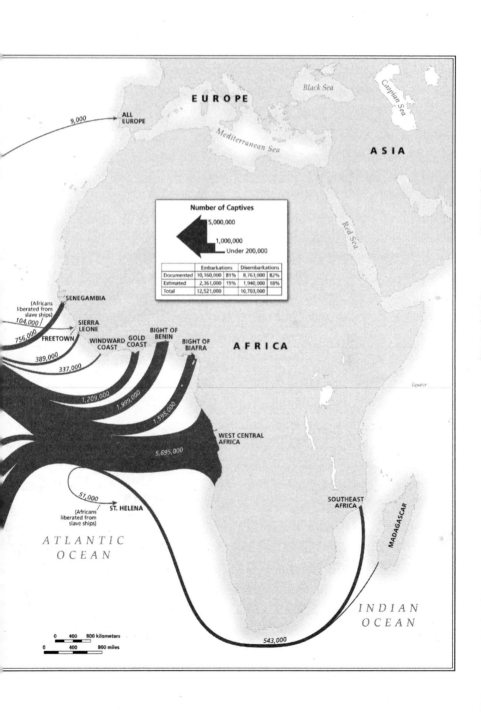

EUROPE

Black Sea

Mediterranean Sea

ASIA

Caspian Sea

Red Sea

Number of Captives

5,000,000

1,000,000

Under 200,000

	Embarkations		Disembarkations	
Documented	10,160,000	81%	8,763,000	82%
Estimated	2,361,000	19%	1,940,000	18%
Total	12,521,000		10,703,000	

9,000 → ALL EUROPE

SENEGAMBIA

(Africans liberated from slave ships) 104,000

SIERRA LEONE

756,000 FREETOWN

389,000

337,000

WINDWARD COAST

GOLD COAST

BIGHT OF BENIN

BIGHT OF BIAFRA

AFRICA

Equator

1,209,000

1,999,000

1,595,000

WEST CENTRAL AFRICA

5,695,000

51,000 ST. HELENA

(Africans liberated from slave ships)

SOUTHEAST AFRICA

MADAGASCAR

ATLANTIC OCEAN

INDIAN OCEAN

543,000

0 400 800 kilometers
0 400 800 miles

Acknowledgements

I am greatly indebted to historians like Lucille Mathurin Mair, Edward Kamau Braithwaite, Barbara Bush, Hilary McD. Beckles, Michael Craton, Richard S. Dunn, Barry Higman, Nicole Phillip, Olive Senior, Monica Schuler, Richard Sheridan, and many others. Their pioneering work in this field paved the way for this modest attempt to explore how African women experienced and resisted slavery in the West Indies.

I have tried to acknowledge all my sources and if any were missed, it was not intentional. My aim was to bring what has been a largely academic debate into the realms of popular history, thereby making this hidden 'her-story' accessible to a wider readership. Hopefully, in the course of time, others will fill in the inevitable gaps and omissions. With so many hidden histories yet to be unearthed, there will always be room for more narratives.

Finally, I am hugely grateful to Beverley Bryan, Heidi Mirza, Suzanne Scafe, Charlotte Ennis, to my uncle, Dr.

Yankum Dadzie, and to friends and colleagues who have read and commented on the manuscript of this book as it evolved. Your feedback has enriched this effort to give voice to countless silenced women. Indeed, it is largely thanks to your support and encouragement that it has finally found its way into print.

Medaase![1]

Stella Dadzie, December 2019

Slavery and the Slave Trade, with its crude levelling of sexual distinctions, meant that African women shared every inch of the man's spiritual and physical odyssey.

Lucille Mathurin Mair (historian)[1]

When they told me my new-born babe was a girl, my heart was heavier than it had ever been before. Slavery is terrible for men; but it is far more terrible for women. Superadded to the burden common to all, they *have wrongs, and sufferings, and mortifications peculiarly their own.*

Harriet Jacobs (African American slave)[2]

As my two estates are at the two extremities of the island, I am entitled to say from my own knowledge . . . that book-keepers and overseers kick black women in the belly from one end of Jamaica to the other.

Matthew 'Monk' Lewis,
Journal of a West India Proprietor (1834)[3]

Introduction: His-story, Her-story

History for the most part has been written by men, for men and thus records largely what men want to see.

Barbara Bush (historian), 1982[1]

My history teacher rationed high marks as if in the midst of a war. This probably explains why the ten out of ten he scrawled beneath my careful little drawing of the Spinning Jenny has stuck so firmly in my memory. 'In 1764', I'd written in my neatest handwriting, 'James Hargreaves invented the Spinning Jenny. It was an improvement on the spinning wheel because it could spin several balls of yarn at the same time, which meant the mills could produce more cotton. Inventions like this contributed to Britain's Industrial Revolution.'

Or words to that effect.

It was 1961 and I was nine years old. In those days, children were expected to quietly copy what was written on the blackboard and underline the most important words in red so we wouldn't forget them. Our teacher, a bulbous-eyed Mr Hode, renowned for his dislike of children, was in the habit of rapping you over the knuckles with a twelve-inch wooden ruler if you forgot this sacred requirement. And if your attention wandered during one of his sermon-like ramblings, his board cleaner, a vicious block of wood lined on one side with felt, would whizz past your ear, trailing a toxic cloud of chalk dust. There was no window gazing or idle doodling in *his* class. If you valued your playtime, you gave him your undivided attention as soon as he strode into the room.

The Toad, as he was dubbed in the playground, terrified me. Aside from his general tyranny, I was the only 'coloured' girl in my class, which made me horribly conspicuous. Yet for some reason, I grew to love history. The bizarre antics of kings (and the occasional queen) must have captured my imagination. Plus, learning about the past, albeit about people who were long since dead, beat geography, hands down. 'Ghana: (capital city Accra): main exports peanuts and cocoa'. Even then, young as I was, that tired old map on the wall with Britain's colonial conquests marked out in pink left me cold.

Instead of battles and general mayhem, the Industrial Revolution turned out to be disappointingly bloodless. A whole lesson was devoted to the curious contraption we were instructed to copy into our exercise books. Yet there was no mention of the fact that Mr Hargreaves's bold new invention relied on a continuous supply of raw cotton; not so much as a whisper about the enforced labour of millions of enslaved and brutalised Africans. The Toad kept quiet about that little piece of the jigsaw. The way he saw it, history was all about Britain and empire. He fed us a diet of glorious white conquest and, in our innocence, we swallowed it whole.

This wasn't just happening in our history classes, though – the entire curriculum was biased. Words like 'primitive' or 'underdeveloped' slipped readily from our teachers' tongues, whatever their subject. Non-white people, if not invisible, were either savage, stupid or irrelevant. The idea that anyone black or non-white might have contributed to our understanding of maths, science or literature was never even considered. Meanwhile, in music, we were encouraged to sing *Rule Britannia* and *Land of Hope and Glory* until we knew the words by heart.

It was a good ten years before I began to understand the link between Mr Hargreaves's Spinning Jenny and the slaves captured a mere stone's throw from the village where my father was born. Like its wars and revolutions, Britain's industrialisation had been presented as a series of unconnected events in which only powerful or infamous white men played any meaningful part. The Toad never once mentioned anyone brown or female like me, and in a world where knowledge and power were so firmly located behind the teacher's desk, who was I to ask why?

It was only with the rise of the American civil rights movement and its more militant alter ego, Black Power, that my understanding of the history I'd been taught began to evolve. I chanced across George Jackson's *Soledad Brother*[2] in a public library one rainy afternoon and became well and truly hooked. Books by Bobby Seale, Malcolm X and (joy of joys!) Angela Davis fed a hunger I didn't even know I'd possessed. I read everything I could lay my hands on, especially history books. But as I searched for the missing pieces of the jigsaw, my suspicions were confirmed. Black people had literally been airbrushed out of the picture.

They were not alone. Feminists like Sheila Rowbotham were busy arguing that women had been 'hidden from history' almost as successfully, while Marx and Engels had long since come to similar conclusions about the working class. Apparently, the names history had chosen to remember were highly selective – more about who wielded the most political clout at the time.[3] No surprise, then, that my efforts to locate black women in this gaping void proved doubly fruitless. If the achievements of working-class white people were peripheral to those of kings and princes, women of African descent with their triple burden of gender, class *and* race hardly got a look-in. I felt a growing urge to name some names, and maybe pour a libation or two to honour their memory.

I was a working mother before I could indulge this sentiment in any meaningful way. Armed with a distant 'O' Level in history class, a sabbatical year at London University's School of Oriental and African Studies gave me the chance to explore at a postgraduate level questions that had been bothering me since primary school. With the writings of men like Franz Fanon, Eric Williams, C. L. R. James and Walter Rodney tucked under my belt,[4] I came armed with a healthy Afrocentric take on the subject and a tendency to side with the underdog. Both proved indispensable.

The challenge, as I saw it then, was to not get sidetracked by all the academic claptrap. My tutors had their clever postmodernist theories to mystify us with, but I could draw from real, lived experience. By then I had visited Saltpond, my father's village in Ghana, and spent time travelling around Jamaica. Nothing about the vibrant, creative people I'd encountered in either country suggested dumb acquiescence. My thesis seemed pretty straightforward: it was the struggles between white masters and black slaves, oppressors and oppressed, that had led to the abolition of the transatlantic slave trade in 1807, and this in turn had paved the way for the slaves' eventual emancipation a quarter of a century later. To credit Wilberforce with this victory, as if he alone were responsible, was like crediting Christopher Columbus with the discovery of America – 'a dyam, blasted lie'.[5]

Of course, the deeper I delved, the more I realised things weren't that simple. To view history in terms of absolutes, whether absolute truths or absolute lies, was to oversimplify a complex set of forces and circumstances that historians, if they are honest, can only ever guess at. It made no sense whatsoever to talk of 'slaves' or 'abolitionists' as homogenous groups who had acted in unison or spoken with a unanimous voice. Even established notions of race, class and gender proved a blur of contradictions. By the end of that sabbatical year, the only conclusion I could embrace with any certainty was that the respective actions of the enslaved and those who championed their emancipation – diverse and disparate as they were – had combined with the economic imperatives of the day to work like a pincer until the abolition of the Africa trade became an increasingly urgent and persuasive option.[6]

I came to realise that studying history was like detective work. However bloodied or one-sided the evidence, it could be interrogated and interpreted in an infinite number of ways. Then as now, lying by omission was common practice, and nowhere was this more apparent than in regard to black and brown-skinned women. The records, diaries, plantation inventories, abolitionist debates, much of the primary evidence, in fact, had either been written, compiled or interpreted by white males who assumed their experience was not only central but all-embracing. So, despite immersing myself in specialist history texts for months on end, my question continued to rankle: in over 400 years of slavery, with all of its documented horrors, what happened to the women?

I soon discovered that a growing number of Afrocentric historians, many of them based in the Caribbean, had been asking the selfsame question – women like Lucille Mathurin Mair, Barbara Bush, Pat Bishop, Erna Brodber, Mavis Campbell, Beverly Carey, Elsa Goveia, Olive Senior, Monica Schuler, Verene Shepherd and Sylvia Wynter, to name a few. Men like Hilary Beckles, Edward Kamau Braithwaite, Richard Sheridan and Michael Craton had also been doing invaluable research in this area. By delving into surviving medical and plantation records, reviewing parliamentary reports and newspaper archives, rereading old diaries and trawling through private letters, they had unearthed insights into the experience of enslaved women that not only challenged prevailing stereotypes but might otherwise never have seen the light of day. Their work has also helped to challenge the notion that the experience of enslaved people in the American South was all-encompassing, for while it was similar in many respects, it was by no means the same.

Thanks to this pioneering research, the extent to which Africa's enslaved peoples were agents in their own emancipation is finally acknowledged, if only in specialist academic circles. How women contributed to this process is also increasingly documented, although the full extent and precise nature of their role is still debated. Strange, then, that over 200 years after abolition, despite this important sea change, our popular media remain fixated on the achievements of a handful of conscience-stricken white men, with the odd black man thrown in for good measure. If Hollywood is to be believed, enslaved people in the Americas owed their freedom to Abraham Lincoln, William Wilberforce and a gun-wielding cowboy named Django.

The realities of ordinary enslaved women have stayed mostly off-screen, and but for the few notable exceptions mentioned earlier, the same has been true of established historical texts on the subject, specifically those written by white male historians. From the earliest European descriptions of intransigent Maroons heading for the hills to latter-day accounts of slave rebellions, black women have been largely conspicuous by their absence. On the rare occasions when they are mentioned, they tend to be viewed through the lens of a depressingly long tradition of academic misogyny, bolstered by some pretty crude and predictable sexual stereotypes. Such perspectives have fuelled the notion of enslaved women as wanton and compliant – exotic mistresses or brazen hussies who pandered willingly to massah's sexual whims, so hopelessly promiscuous that (ironically) they had no time left to breed. Today's black 'hoes and bitches', in other words, whose enduring appeal is all too evident in music, fashion and endless popular media productions.

Competing with the idea that women had it easier under slavery because they spent so much of it on their backs is the equally dubious notion of the long-suffering, broad-backed matriarch, eminently suited to the rigours of slavery on account of her African ancestry. Archetypal mother figure, she seems capable of overcoming all odds, stoically raising her brood of fatherless children with barely a murmur of complaint. This idealised, one-dimensional image takes scant account of the complexity of the different rankings and functions of enslaved women, much less the range and sophistication of their responses. Like all stereotypes, it relies on a kernel of truth; but by buying into it wholesale, we risk losing sight of many alternative narratives.

With little historical identity beyond these two limited roles, it is small wonder that the nameless female casualties of plantation violence come across as little more than passive onlookers. It's as if enslaved women were somehow caught up by default in confrontations from which only men could emerge as heroes. With very few exceptions (and we could literally count them on the fingers of one hand), enslaved women who fought back have been relegated to the role of invisible camp followers.

His-story has a convenient and highly selective memory, this much we know, but if we sift through the evidence, a far more complex picture begins to emerge. The canvas may be worn, the paint may be cracked and faded, but there are women in the foreground and they do *not* look happy. Look closer and you'll see them more clearly. Their bodies are bent, their feet callused and swollen. They are menstruating, giving birth, collapsing from fatigue and dying from abuse or hideous diseases. Across their backs, thick keloid scars are clearly visible, as are the suppurating wounds left by brandings, collars and leg irons. The few who are clothed sport dark sweat stains under their armpits. Some look half-crazed with the horror of it all, some seem resigned to the prospect of an untimely death. But others are watching, waiting, biding their time, plotting their escape or dreaming of revenge. Occasionally the glint of a weapon or a barely concealed vial of poison hints at more ominous practices.

Against this backdrop of unrelenting misery, some women have found ways to make their lives more tolerable. At first glance, they do not look like women who would willingly trade their bodies for trinkets or treats. Without doubt, there are some favoured concubines among them, women who have learnt to play the few cards they were dealt by opting to collude or comply. They stand haughty and erect, ever mindful of their perilous status. Yet those who seek favour rather than endure the miserable fate of their mothers and grandmothers are in a distinct minority. The numbers speak for themselves, they are the exception to the rule.

Move closer and our picture becomes even more intriguing. Away from the fields, some women can be seen dusting the silver or waiting at table with lowered eyes and pricked ears. Others are busy hauling produce to market or hiring out their skills as cooks, seamstresses, laundresses, nurses and midwives. Their mobility is a godsend, particularly for those with clandestine messages or overheard news to relay. A handful of female entrepreneurs, having acquired or purchased their freedom, have opened lodging houses, supplementing their precarious income by administering to the sick or tending to the needs of passing travellers. With their keen, well-tuned ears, they too have a role to play in this vast, subversive grapevine.

A majority of the women are toiling in the fields and mill-houses. Many have an angry glint in their eyes as they feed the huge rollers or squint skyward at the merciless sun. Beyond them, in the distant mountains and forests, hard to detect in the dense foliage, we may even catch the occasional tantalising glimpse of a female Maroon – proud, ferocious women, so intent on a self-determined life that they prefer the risk of a brutal death to the prospect of recapture.

With this more nuanced image of female resistance in mind, it cannot be right that their historical legacy is so one-dimensional. As the planter 'Monk' Lewis observed, black women were 'kicked in the belly' throughout the period of slavery. Yet in many ways, these women's response can be seen as a metaphorical kick in the belly for those who tried and failed to dehumanise them. To deny them their rightful place in history simply adds insult to a 400-year-long injury.

To some, the case for letting sleeping dogs lie must seem quite persuasive, no doubt because the subject of slavery is deemed too uncomfortable to warrant such scrutiny. Whisper the S-word on this side of the pond and, bar a handful of guilt-stricken universities, there is a collective squirm of embarrassment in the national seat. Mention reparations and politicians fudge or grow defensive. African Caribbean pupils have even been known to complain when the subject is brought up in class, suggesting little under-standing of their roots, much less pride in their impressive heritage. Meanwhile, most of us turn an indifferent eye to growing evidence that modern-day slavery is alive, kicking and operating under our very noses.

But this is precisely *why* the subject of slavery and the slave trade remains relevant. Despite the enduring myth of a self-contained 'black' history, events in Africa and the Caribbean did not take place on another planet. Nor were the beneficiaries of slavery confined to mainland America, as recent films and much of the available literature tend to suggest. Britain's imperial past is inextricably linked to the contributions and sacrifices of the enslaved. Her towns and cities are littered with evidence that for hundreds of years, African blood, sweat and tears oiled the wheels of this country's progress and lined its citizens' pockets with gold. It was her enslaved and colonised subjects who helped put the 'Great' in Great Britain, yet the great British public remains largely in denial.

There are other reasons why the realities of the trans-atlantic slave trade warrant closer attention. 'A people without knowledge of their past history, origin and culture is like a tree without roots', to quote Marcus Garvey, and in a society like ours, where home-grown ethnic diversity is increasingly the norm, his argument has never rung truer. Today, with thousands of African women risking life and limb to make the hazardous trek north under conditions not dissimilar to the middle passage, the continuities are stark. So, however painful, however shameful, a better understanding of our shared past is vital to the health of Britain's evolving multicultural identity.

Stories of how Africans and their descendants survived the experience of enslavement with their dignity and humanity intact provide a vast, untapped source of national pride. Like the survivors of the Holocaust who populated London's East End or the heroes and she-roes who resisted fascism during the Second World War, their courage and resilience deserve to be honoured, their intrepid acts publicly revered. If even a handful of African Caribbean pupils feel shame or unease at the mention of slavery, something has gone seriously wrong.

The enslavement of Africans by Europeans was, without question, one of the worst crimes ever perpetrated against humanity. Back in 2007, the 200th anniversary of the parliamentary act to abolish the British slave trade provided a rare (and largely missed) opportunity to highlight the role of its victims in bringing about its eventual demise. To have allowed that moment to pass without raising the profile of women was an added travesty. It's time to place women centre stage where they belong, fist in glove with the men.

It was a long and arduous journey from slavery to freedom, but there is growing evidence to suggest that women were present every step of the way. A cornerstone of the plantation economy and increasingly the very key to its survival, enslaved women's contribution to its eventual demise remains one of history's best-kept secrets.

Aside from Mary Prince's transcribed narrative, which the pro-slavery lobby did everything in their power to discredit,[7] enslaved West Indian women had few opportunities to record their stories for posterity. Yet from their dusty footprints and the umpteen small clues they left for us to unravel, there's no question that they earned their place in history. From Jamaica to Barbados, Haiti to Trinidad, the emerging picture is compelling. Pick any Caribbean island

and you'll find race, skin colour and rank interacting with gender in a unique and often volatile way. Moreover, the evidence points to a distinctly female role in the development of a culture of slave resistance – a role that was not just central, but downright dynamic.

Enslaved women found ways of fighting back that beggar belief. Whether responding to the horrendous conditions of plantation life, the sadistic vagaries of their captors or the 'peculiar burdens of their sex', their collective sanity relied on a highly subversive adaptation of the values and cultures they smuggled with them naked from different parts of Africa. By sustaining or adapting remembered cultural practices – be it music, storytelling, preparing food, administering medicines, fixing hair, birthing and naming rites or rituals for burying their dead – they ensured that the lives of chattel slaves retained both meaning and purpose. This sense of self gave rise to a sense of agency so that over time, both their subtle acts of insubordination and their conscious acts of rebellion came to undermine the very fabric and survival of West Indian slavery.

In a nutshell, as this book sets out to show, enslaved women made a distinctly *female* contribution to the advancement of the struggle for freedom – a contribution that deserves to be remembered, acknowledged and honoured across the African diaspora.

Gang of female slaves, central Africa, nineteenth-century engraving (Getty images).

A Terrible Crying:
Women and the Africa Trade

There were many women who filled the air with heart-rending cries which could hardly be drowned by the drums.

Ship's surgeon, 1693

There is no way to tell this horror story in a palatable way. Perhaps, if the descendants of those who benefited most had made recompense for this dark chapter in our shared history, it would be easier to talk about. But the legacies of those centuries of genocide and abuse are still with us, in relative levels of poverty and education, infant mortality and prison occupancy rates, wars, human suffering and a plethora of other glaring North-South inequalities, both social and economic, that cry out for reparation.

For all of this, it was never a straightforward black-white issue, and who owes what to whom is an ongoing debate. The trade in captured Africans was a complex transaction and Europeans were responsible for every aspect of its execution, yet the unpalatable truth is that it could never have survived or prospered without significant African involvement. But if some Africans colluded in the theft and sale of their own people, the evidence shows that there were also countless others who found the courage and the means to fight back, despite every effort to quash their human spirit.

This is the thought that preoccupies me as I step down into the dungeons of Elmina Castle in Ghana, Portugal's first African trading fort. Built in 1482, it is an enduring monument to one of history's most shameful epochs. In the holding cells, more than two centuries after Britain officially abolished the Atlantic slave trade, the stench of hundreds of thousands of captives still clings to the walls.

In the sun-scorched courtyard, a solitary cannonball too heavy to lift marks the start of our guided tour. Our guide describes how women who declined to 'entertain' their captors during the long months awaiting embarkation would be chained to the cannonball at the ankle or forced to hold it aloft in the blistering heat for hours at a time – a tantalising hint of the defiant mindset of those recently captured women. Inside the death cell, where mutinous soldiers and rebellious captives alike were left to rot, the atmosphere remains oppressive. Its door, marked with a skull and crossbones, acts like the lid of a coffin, blocking out light and air. Yet even this tomb-like cell speaks of dissent and rebellion – why else would it have existed?

A narrow, well-worn staircase leads us from the courtyard to the officers' quarters above. The windows offer a panoramic view of the Atlantic Ocean, evoking a distant memory of slave ships of every nation anchored offshore, plying their ignominious trade. The governor's breezy rooms contrast starkly with the suffocating gloom of the slave holes below, where the claw marks of the desperate and the dying are still visible above a dark, indelible tidemark of human waste. The horrors endured by hundreds of tightly packed captives receive graphic illustration when our guide points to the former site of huge 'necessary tubs' that would have been filled to the brim with excrement. A vile death by drowning awaited those unfortunate souls who, too exhausted to perch on the edge, slipped and fell in.

We stoop low to enter the cramped corridor that led countless men, women and children to step, bound and shackled, through the 'door of no return'. The architecture tells its own story – a narrow, single-file opening, designed to frustrate all thoughts of escape as the captives were bundled into longboats that would ferry them to the waiting ships. Yet thoughts of escape there must have been, for a whole industry was developed to equip the traders with the heavy iron chains and shackles they needed in order to prevent it.

Back in the courtyard, we are almost blinded by the brilliant sunshine reflecting from a brass plaque in honour of the millions who perished. It reads: 'In Everlasting Memory of the anguish of our ancestors. May those who died rest in peace. May those who return find their roots. May humanity never again perpetrate such injustice against humanity. We, the living, vow to uphold this'.

Fine words indeed.

Conditions such as those in Elmina would become commonplace as local chieftains became more and more complicit in the capture and sale of their own people. During the seventeenth century, their efforts to consolidate local or regional power came to depend increasingly on the exchange of prisoners of war and other hapless victims, both male and female, in return for guns and sought-after European commodities. The result was a highly lucrative partnership – one that has survived to this day in the corrupt dealings between the power brokers of Africa and Europe.

As people-trade entrenched itself along the West African coast as far south as the Congo and Angola, those intrepid Portuguese, Danish, Dutch, French and English traders, many of whom built their own forts and trading posts, could rely on a steady supply of captives from the interior to fill the waiting barracoons – the end result of a complex process of barter and exchange of 'equivalent' goods in return for captured humans. Increasingly, African lives came to be valued in beads, cloth, gunpowder, rum and iron bars.

Not all chiefs took so readily to the sale of their own people. Particularly in the early years of the trade, when the slavers' success relied heavily on the patronage of local rulers, some chiefs bucked the trend and resisted all involvement. Africa, like Europe, was no more than a vague geographical concept at the time. In reality, Europe's slave traders encountered a complex array of kingdoms and tribes, some more sophisticated than others, with competing interests, language barriers, social and cultural differences, rivalries and territorial ambitions, as well as widely differing attitudes to slavery. Inevitably they met with powerful Africans who wanted a piece of the action.

But they also found others who were vehemently opposed the trade, including some impressive African women.

As early as 1701, the Royal African Company was writing to its factors at Cape Coast castle to alert them to the dangers of local resistance, led by a woman who clearly wielded considerable power in her own right:

> We are informed of a Negro Woman that has some influence in the country, and employs it always against our Influence, one Taggeba; this you must inspect and prevent in the best Methods you can and least Expense.[1]

Taggeba was one of several powerful African women who resisted European encroachment in the early seventeenth century. Ana Nzinga, queen of the Ndongo (c. 1581–1663) was an equally formidable opponent, a fearsome woman who remained a flea in the ear of the Portuguese throughout her thirty-year reign. As well as keeping a harem of both male and female consorts, she is said to have dressed in men's clothing and insisted on being called 'king' rather than 'queen'.

Her brazen, imperious character is legendary. During her first encounter with colonial governor Correia de Sousa, she is said to have refused his offer of a seat on the floor, ordering one of her servants to get down on his hands and knees instead to form a chair. Later, under the pretence of forming an alliance with them, she allowed herself to be baptised Dona Ana de Souza and learnt the Portuguese language. Distrusted by the Portuguese for her habit of harbouring escapees and much feared for her military prowess when resisting European intrusion, she point-blank refused to become their puppet and was never effectively subdued.[2]

Even though resistance to European traders was sporadic and mercilessly repressed, it persisted in some form or another for centuries. Their names may have been lost to us, yet women are known to have played a significant role militarily, spiritually and politically. Several historical accounts confirm the influence of African women as leaders and warriors: Amina or Aminata (d. 1610), the warrior Hausa queen of Zazzau (modern-day Zaria), led an army of over 20,000 in her wars of expansion and surrounded her city with defensive walls that are known to this day as *ganuwar amina* or 'Amina's walls'. Described in Hausa praise songs as 'a woman as capable as a man', she reigned for over thirty-five years.[3]

There was also Beatriz Kimpa Vita (1684–1706) of the Congo, who insisted that Jesus was an African and whose call to Congolese unity was taken as a direct challenge to the designs of European slavers and missionaries. Burnt at the stake as a heretic together with her infant son, her spiritual influence spread so far and wide that enslaved Haitians used the words from one of her prayers as a rallying cry when they rose in rebellion almost a century later.[4]

Over 200 years after Ana Nzinga's rule, warrior queen Yaa Asantewaa came to embody this spirit of female resistance when, as the chosen leader of the Ashanti in their struggle against British colonialism, she denounced her fellow chiefs for allowing their king, the Asantehene, to be seized and exiled. In her words:

> Now I have seen that some of you fear to go forward to fight for our king. If it were the brave days of Osei Tutu, Okomfo Anokye and Opuku Ware I, chiefs would not

sit down to see their king taken without firing a shot. No white man could have dared to speak to the Chief of Asante in the way the governor spoke to you chiefs this morning. Is it true that the bravery of Asante is no more? I cannot believe it, it cannot be! I must say this: if you, the men of Asante, will not go forward, then we will. I shall call upon my fellow women. We will fight the white men. We will fight till the last of us falls on the battlefield.[5]

Yaa Asantewaa, born in 1840, would have been around sixty when she was elected to lead an army of 5,000 in the Ashanti war of resistance against the British at the turn of the twentieth century. Described by the British as 'the soul and head of the whole rebellion', she is thought to have been the mother or aunt of a chief who had been sent into exile with the king. Although she was eventually defeated and exiled herself, she remains a Ghanaian national she-ro and a figure of inspiration to this day for her refusal to bow down to colonial rule.

This is not to suggest that recalcitrant men didn't play an equally important role in resisting the theft of their people. In 1720, Tomba, chief of the Baga, attempted to organise an alliance of popular resistance that would drive the traders and their agents into the sea. The Oba (kings) of Benin are also reputed to have been opposed to the trade for many years.[6] King Agaja II of Dahomey, whose reign lasted from 1718 to 1740, is said to have been so incensed by the incursion of traders into his kingdom that he raised an army of intrepid women to help resist them. A letter, thought to have been dictated and sent by Agaja to the English king, George II, in 1731, even went so far as to propose an alternative scheme of trade, substituting the export of human beings with exports of home-grown sugar, cotton and indigo.[7]

On second thought, King Agaja may not be the best example of male agency. His palace was 'a virtual city of women, experienced in the mechanics of government' – close to 8,000 women, whose roles included blocking or promoting outsiders' interests. Said to have exercised choice, influence and autonomy, they wielded considerable authority and power. This ferocious army of Amazonian 'soldieresses' was legendary both for the warriors' physical prowess and their elevated status. They called themselves *N'nonmiton* ('our mothers') and others saw them as elite, aloof and untouchable.

As bodyguards to the king, they were trained to display speed, courage and physical endurance on the battlefield, and expected to fight to the death to protect him. Their fearsome, ruthless legacy is remembered to this day.[8]

There were other kings who resisted, too. According to Carl Bernard Wadstrom, who made a voyage to the coast of Guinea in 1787, the King of Almammy was so opposed to the trade that he enacted a law forbidding the transport of slaves through his territory. Wadstrom was an eyewitness when the king returned gifts sent by the Senegal Company in an attempt to win him over, declaring that 'all the riches of that company would not divert him from his design'. Even toward the end of the eighteenth century, by which time the trade was well entrenched, the inhabitants of the Grain Coast were known both for their reluctance to trade in slaves and their habit of attacking European slavers who attempted it.

Sadly, back in Europe, such protests fell on deaf ears. After all, why concern themselves with the plight of Africans when there were such huge profits to be made? Aside from copious supplies of rum and gin, which created their own dependency, one of the most lucrative exports to Africa at the time was guns. Between August 1713 and May 1715, the Royal African Company ordered no less than 11,986 fusees, pistols, muskets and Jamaica guns for export to the Guinea coast,[9] the latter made specifically for the slave trade and known for their habit of exploding the first time they were fired.[10] King Tegbesu of Dahomey (King Agaja's successor) is said to have complained bitterly that a consignment of English guns had exploded when used, injuring many of his soldiers. In 1765, a fairly typical year, 150,000 guns were exported to Africa from Birmingham alone – the beginnings of an ignominious arms trade that has killed or maimed millions of Africans and has continued unchecked into the twenty-first century.

Before long, power and guns would become inextricably linked, with the price of a slave costing anything from one to five guns, depending on the location of the sale. Soon captive Africans, typically prisoners of war, had replaced gold, ivory, pepper and redwood as the primary currency. Meanwhile, resident European factors, whose 'palavers' with less scrupulous local rulers left them well placed to stir up local rivalries, were often charged with deliberately fomenting unrest in a cynical move to increase demand for guns and the resulting supply of captives.

The truth is although it was Europeans who organised the triangular trade in their scramble for profit and influence, they could not have done so without co-opting some extremely power-hungry Africans. The collusion of chiefs and indigenous traders was the inevitable by-product of a system that thrived on avarice. Elmina, like hundreds of other forts and trading posts along the West African coast, would soon become a busy commercial hub, its predominantly European occupants dependent on local communities for water, fresh food, transport and, in some cases, even armed protection.

Bogus treaties with local chiefs may have given Europe's traders an initial foot in the door, but their success – and, on some occasions, their very survival – came to rely on the services of local people: boatmen, domestic servants, messengers, traders, brokers, interpreters and so-called 'wenches'. For them and their descendants, this trade in fellow humans would ultimately become a way of life. Treacherous currents and diseases that could devastate an entire crew encouraged European ships to anchor far offshore for their own safety. The trade would have died an early death but for the expertise of local boatmen, who were handsomely rewarded for ferrying people and goods to and from the waiting ships. If they were fortunate enough to escape capture themselves, it was only because their skills in handling the canoes, sometimes as long as eighty feet and able to carry over 100 people, were vital to the endless traffic between ship and shore.

Within 200 years, what began as a Portuguese monopoly in 1490 had become a free-for-all. As the British, French, Danish, Dutch, Prussians, Spanish and Swedish jostled with the Portuguese for strategic dominance of the coastal forts and supply routes, competition was fierce, often deadly. Elmina Castle, seized by the Dutch in 1642, changed hands several times until finally, over two centuries later, it fell under British control. A similar fate befell Cape Coast Castle, Anomabu and many other forts and trading posts, 100 of which had been built on the Gold Coast alone. Meanwhile, in the Americas, the establishment of plantations for growing sugar, tobacco, cotton, rice, coffee and other produce led to a declining interest in Africa's gold reserves and an ever-growing demand for 'black ivory'. This steady drain of men and women, paupers and princesses alike, would deplete the continent's most precious resource for centuries to come. Africa is, as we know, still in recovery.

To begin with, back in Europe, the traffic in human lives provoked few moral qualms. Initially characterised by mutual curiosity and respect, relationships between Africans and Europeans only began to change once the trade became established. Slavery was a lot easier to defend if its victims could be vilified, and the justifications, however crude, were easily swallowed by Europe's illiterate masses. Africans, it was argued, were 'slaves by nature', little more than apes or talking parrots, a savage, godless race whose 'impudent nakedness' was proof of their inherent immorality. To enslave them, therefore, was seen as an act of salvation, for it saved them from themselves. By the end of the eighteenth century, an entire racist mythology had been devised to justify African enslavement, couched in lofty, pseudo-scientific language and sanctioned by both church and state.

The extent to which Africans were dehumanised is apparent from the earliest Portuguese references to the shipment of slaves by the tonne and records of their transportation across the Atlantic like so many heads of cattle. It can be no coincidence that in Portuguese, 'to explore' and 'to exploit' are one and the same word (*explorar*). The Royal African Company was quick to follow suit. Bankrolled by wealthy patrons, it supplied nearly 50,000 slaves to the British West Indies between 1680 and 1688 alone.[11] It would be another 120 years before Britain publicly condemned the tyranny of the transatlantic trade and the 'great enormities . . . practised in Africa and upon the persons of its inhabitants, by the subjects of different European Powers'.[12]

The enormities were great indeed, regardless of gender. African women are prominent in the accounts of contemporary eyewitnesses and in their detailed, hand-drawn sketches of the coffle line. Secured by wooden yokes fashioned from forked tree branches that could weigh as much as seven kilos, they can be seen leading children by the hand and carrying goods or supplies. Francis Moore, factor to the Royal African Company between 1730 and 1735, recorded seeing caravans of up to 2,000 slaves tied by the neck with leather thongs in batches of thirty or forty, 'having generally a Bundle of Corn, or an Elephant's Tooth upon each of their heads'.[13]

For those seized inland, the trek from the forested interior could mean walking several hundred miles in the pitiless heat. How many Africans perished before reaching the coast can never be quantified but it is thought that close to half of them – as many as 12 million people – may have perished before they even reached the coast, either from escape attempts, wounds sustained during capture, summary execution or sheer exhaustion. In such desperate circumstances, suicide was probably one of the few available acts of resistance. Many a captive is said to have chosen death by their own hand over the trauma of being driven like cattle toward an uncertain fate.

Flogging was common practice on the coffle line, with no exception made for young children or pregnant women. Babies, the elderly or the infirm, viewed as an unnecessary encumbrance, were often abandoned en route or casually murdered. In fact, the Royal African Company tacitly encouraged such practices. In an early missive to the King of Whydah in 1701, it insisted that the company was not interested in anyone 'above 30 years of age nor lower than four and a half feet high . . . nor none Sickly deformed or defective in Body or Limb . . . And ye Diseased and ye Aged'. A year later, a letter to their newly appointed agent, Dalby Thomas, included written instructions to procure 'as many Boys and Girls as possible', ideally in their early teens, and to avoid sending 'old Negroes'.[14]

Rumours of these atrocities must have spread like wildfire. Deep in the interior, talking drums, which could convey news over hundreds of miles in the space of a few hours, and the tales of itinerant traders ensured that the slavers' terrifying reputation preceded them. Explorer Vernon Cameron, who witnessed a passing slave caravan while travelling in central Africa in the mid-nineteenth century, described how, at its approach, the local people 'immediately bolted into the village and closed the entrances'. Camped close to the path, he watched as 'the whole caravan passed on in front, the mournful procession lasting more than two hours. Women and children, foot-sore and overburdened, were urged on unremittingly by their barbarous masters; and even when they reached their camp it was no haven of rest for the poor creatures.

They were compelled to fetch water, cook, build huts and collect firewood for those who owned them'.[15] Whether these captives were headed for Portuguese traders off the coast of Angola or the Arab slave markets to the north is not known, since both continued to operate long after the Atlantic trade was outlawed by the British. Either way, on the arduous journey still ahead of them, women were clearly expected to bear the brunt of the hardship.[16]

Mungo Park, who accompanied a slave coffle in Senegal toward the end of the eighteenth century, witnessed the miseries of the Atlantic-bound coffle first-hand, including the substitution of an enslaved man who was too sick to travel with a young village girl encountered en route. His description of her anguish on learning her fate suggests that however ignorant of their eventual destination, the captives were only too aware of the horrors that lay ahead:

> Never was a face of serenity more suddenly changed into one of the deepest distress. The terror which she manifested on having the load put upon her head and the rope fastened around her neck, and the sorrow with which she bade adieu to her companions were truly affecting.[17]

As demand for slaves increased, the King of Whydah and other local chiefs tried securing supplies to order, mostly by means of armed raids. Not all captives were prisoners of war, however. People could be sold into slavery for a variety of reasons: debt, witchcraft, theft, adultery, non-payment of a tribute, incurring their chief's displeasure or simply having no means to support themselves. Others, like Olaudah

Equiano and his 'dear sister' were simply in the wrong place at the wrong time and found themselves kidnapped.

Women and girls were especially vulnerable, it seems. The female relatives of male felons, mothers who gave birth to twins, family servants, even young girls who menstruated earlier than normal risked being despatched into slavery to meet the ever-growing demand. In 1694, Captain Thomas Phillips reported that, when slaves were in short supply, the king would 'often . . . sell 300 or 400 of his wives to complete their number'. On the Ivory Coast, perhaps in the hope of taking the pressure off themselves, the Avikam people stole or purchased large numbers of female slaves with a view to breeding and selling the children to the Europeans. Whatever their motives, the incentives for African suppliers must have been significant. And since guns, which represented both power and security, could only be acquired in exchange for captives, they were caught in a double bind.

Inevitably some ships' captains, especially 'ten percenters' who were backed by private investors, chose to bypass the company. During periods of shortfall, when ships languished off the coast, unable to leave, kidnapping became an increasingly popular course of action. Crew members, usually confined to their quarters in a futile effort to contain the spread of disease, would then be expected to play a more active role. The sailors, many of them press-ganged into service themselves, would have been skilled in the art of people-theft. When abolitionist Thomas Clarkson interviewed twenty-two men about their involvement in the Guinea trade, one of his witnesses admitted that 'the Europeans who frequent the coast of Africa do not hesitate to steal the natives whenever an opportunity is offered them'. His witness goes on to describe how 'a very considerable number of the natives of Africa annually become slaves, either by being way-laid and stolen, or decoyed from home under false pretences, and then seized and sold'.[18]

With a local guide and sufficient armed men, the business of procuring slaves could easily bypass the middlemen. Ironically, ordinary Africans had no choice but to take steps to avoid capture by carrying weapons themselves. Others formed defensive alliances with nearby villages or relocated away from those areas most vulnerable to attack. Faced with the constant threat of raids, some villagers developed their own alarm systems. One of Clarkson's informants had been present when several ships' captains 'determined to make a descent on a village at night for the purpose of getting slaves . . . (and) take all they could lay their hands on'. Their attempt was thwarted by a woman who, on seeing them enter her hut, 'shrieked aloud and made a terrible crying'.

Thanks to this woman's warning, the villagers regrouped and fought back until the raiding party, several of whom were killed or wounded in the skirmish, 'fled without precipitation into the water'. But they did not leave empty-handed. While making their escape, five women were seized and taken back to the ship for transportation. The captured women appear to have survived the journey, for they were 'carried to the West Indies, and the port being just opened at South Carolina, they were sold there'.[19]

Women and girls were probably seen as easy targets. Another of Clarkson's informants had been present when 'two black traders informed the Captain . . . that they would procure him two women slaves, if he would assist them in doing it. The Captain accordingly sent Mr — with them to a distance . . . of some miles from the ship. The two young women were . . . brought down, but under the pretence of seeing a relation at Suggery Bay to the windward of Cape Mount. When they had been enticed under this pretence to the water's edge, they were ordered to be swum off on board the (ship's) boat in a very heavy surf, each of the women between two men. When they were put on board the ship they were treacherously sold for slaves.'[20]

Few accounts have survived by those on the receiving end of such trickery, and none of them by women. Abu-Bakr al-Siddiq, born in 1790 in Timbuktu, was one of a literate minority who could record the details of his capture in writing, so he speaks for the silenced, both male and female alike. His captors, he said,

> tore off my clothes, bound me with ropes, gave me a heavy load to carry. They sold me to the Christians and I was bought by a certain captain of a ship at that time. He sent me to a boat, and delivered me over to one of his sailors. The boat immediately pushed off and I was carried on board of the ship. We continued on board ship, at sea, for three months and then came on shore in the land of Jamaica. This was the beginning of my slavery until this day. I tasted the bitterness of slavery from them, and its oppressiveness![21]

Captives who were not taken directly on board could be confined in the coastal forts or 'barracoons' for months at a time. Elmina bears witness to the many thousands who languished in filthy, overcrowded holding cells or slave pens until loaded onto ships that, if they survived the journey, would transport them to the Americas. The dehumanising process began long before embarkation. Yet despite the terrifying consequences, there is evidence that women played an active part in barracoon insurrections during the long months spent awaiting embarkation. Women were almost certainly among those who attempted a rebellion on Bence Island, 'armed only with [their] irons and chains'.[22] They also resisted in other ways, as the solitary cannonball in Elmina Castle bears witness.

Keeping in mind the evocative images of the coffle line and the barracoons, it's worth remembering that by no means all African women who encountered European men did so in shackles. In the coastal fortresses and trading posts, despite phenomenally high mortality rates, some Europeans survived disease, foreign bombardment, political intrigue or the effects of excessive alcohol consumption long enough to form intimate relationships with local women. In fact, the promise of copious sex, typically with young girls, was probably one of the attractions used to lure them overseas. At Cape Coast Castle, just up the coast from Elmina, it was common practice to supply newly arrived officers with an African 'wench' to serve as cook, maid and bed warmer.[23] Similarly, in settlements around the estuary of the River Sierra Leone, it was said that 'every man hath his whore'.[24]

Polygamous arrangements were commonplace, mimicking local practices. During a visit in 1694, Thomas Phillips, a ship's captain, described the European habit of taking

African mistresses as 'a pleasant way of marrying, for they can turn them on and off and take others at pleasure'. This, he observed somewhat smugly, 'makes (the women) very careful to humour their husbands, in washing their linen, cleaning their chambers &c, &c. and the charge of keeping them is little or nothing'.[25] Some of these women may have been willing victims. Others – like the 'Shanti beautee', purchased for around £21 in equivalent goods when her male owner, the governor, died; or 'DM's lady', who was 'sent off the coast' in similar circumstances – found that their favoured status offered them no guarantee of any long-term security.

Relationships with local women were typically casual or short-lived, though some clearly weren't. Officers' wills, letters and other surviving records suggest that marriages at Cape Coast Castle, while not recognised in British law, conformed largely to local customs by requiring payment of a dowry to the girl's mother and a monthly allowance. This practice was not confined to the British. In his letters home, Paul Erdmann Isert, chief surgeon to the Danish in Christiansborg, Accra, from 1783 to 1786, declared that 'one of the most peculiar customs here is the marriage of the Europeans to the daughters of the country'. He went on to describe how 'a Black woman is paid one thaler monthly and a Mulatto woman two thaler monthly by their husbands, and . . . given clothing twice a year'. Not only was this payment for services rendered viewed as an entitlement, but when a woman found herself wedded to a 'ne'er-do-well', she had the right to complain. By way of recompense, her allowance would either be deducted at source from the man's wages or his wages paid over to the woman in their entirety, for her to manage on his behalf.[26]

Isert also described how 'the new husband can send his wife packing the next day if he feels like it', implying that some European men were happy to exploit these arrangements to suit their own sexual appetite. Even so, it is clear that some of these relationships endured. At Cape Coast, Officer Miles arranged for monthly payments be made to his 'Mulattoe Girl' Jamah for over three years, possibly longer, from May 1776, suggesting more than a casual fling. Similarly, on his death in May 1795, Thomas Mitchell left his woman, Nance, the princely sum of twenty pounds, to be paid in gold dust, plus two gold rings 'in consideration of her strict attention and attendance on me during the three years we have lived together'.

Occasionally – perhaps more often than was admitted – such unions led to genuine mutual affection. James Phipps, who was a governor of the castle early in the eighteenth century, is said to have implored his 'mulatto' wife, who bore him several children, to return with him to England. She refused the offer but allowed him to take their four children there to be educated. Another governor, Irishman Richard Brew, fathered seven children with the same woman before returning home in the 1790s.[27] His contemporary, Dutchman Jan Neizer, having married a local woman called Aba, was apparently so content with his lot that he built her a grand house and named it 'Harmonie'.

For some powerful local women, many of whom were slave owners or traders in their own right, political or commercial interests were probably a more pressing consideration than love and affection. The Queen of Winneba, who took the Royal African Company's chief factor, Nicholas Buckeridge, as her lover, probably had more pragmatic motives. Further north, the formidable Senhora Doll, a member of the influential Ya Kumba family, was no doubt securing her interests, too, when she agreed to marry Thomas Corker of Falmouth, the company's last factor. Known as 'the Duchess of Sherbro' by the European slave captains she entertained, she and her descendants went on to establish a small standing army of free Africans, maintaining control over a strategic stretch of land along the banks of the river Sherbro.[28]

Casting all African women as victims obscures the fact that relationships with European men, however short-lived or precarious, offered their concubines a degree of financial security that their wives back in Europe would have envied. Moreover, some women made a lucrative living from the trade. In the Bissagos Islands off Cape Verde, where an earlier preference for male captives had created a large female majority, women controlled most of the transactions. The children resulting from their liaisons with European men populated numerous offshore islands and coastal towns. Rarely acknowledged by the fathers, their Euro-African offspring would eventually become a trading force in their own right, known as *caboceers*. By straddling the cultural and linguistic divide between Europeans and Africans, both sons and daughters acquired increasing power and status, the latter often mentioned in surviving documents as wives, mistresses or favoured 'wenches'.

One such woman was Betsy Heard, the daughter of a liaison between a Liverpool trader and a local woman. Schooled in England, she returned home to inherit her father's trading assets and subsequently rose to prominence as a dealer in slaves along the banks of the River Bereira. By 1794, she had established a monopoly on trade in the area. As owner of the main wharf in Bereira, including a warehouse and several trading ships, she wielded sufficient influence to act as mediator in a long-standing dispute between the Sierra Leone Company and local chiefs, who are said to have regarded her as a queen.[29]

The patronage of chiefs and the mediation of *caboceers* would become vital to Europe's traders, as the theft of Africa's people became entrenched. Procuring and enslaving captive Africans could be a slow and laborious business, especially when competing with faster or better-stocked ships. Once the local market became flooded with cheap European goods, the cost of 'black ivory' increased and the supply of captured Africans began to dwindle. In 1764, Captain Miller of the *Black Prince* complained that he'd waited six months for his agent to acquire just twenty slaves. And when the *Pearl*, which sailed out of Bristol in 1790, had to wait over nine months in Old Calabar for a viable cargo, both the crew and their captives suffered high mortality rates before they could set sail.[30] Many a captive perished in the disease-ridden holds of ships as they languished off the coast, waiting for the quota to be filled. Others endured the prolonged torture of captivity for months, forced to lie spoon-like in their own excrement, vomit or menstrual blood until the ships were fully loaded.

Selection for sale involved detailed and intimate inspection, with specially appointed ships' 'surgeons' examining 'every part of every one of them, to the smallest member, men and women being stark naked'.[31] Captain Phillips recorded an account of one such transaction in his diary. 'Our surgeon', he wrote, 'is forced to examine the privities of both men and women with the nicest scrutiny'.[32] It was also common practice for captives to be branded on the shoulder or breast with a hot iron, to ensure that they could be readily identified by their purchasers. Their suppurating wounds would have been magnets for infection.

Cruelties like this went with the territory. Traders were not averse to beating or murdering those captives who, on account of 'being . . . defective in their limbs, eyes or teeth; or grown grey, or . . . [victims of] the venereal disease, or any other imperfection' were rejected by ships' captains and other European buyers. It is doubtful that any concessions were made to women. These paragons of European civilisation simply turned away when 'traders frequently beat those Negroes which are objected to by the captains and use them with great severity . . . Instances have happened . . . that the traders have dropped their canoes under the stern of the vessel and instantly beheaded them in sight of the captain'.[33]

Of course, brutality is not confined to any one race. It never has been. Both Africans and Europeans were guilty of such atrocities, reflecting contemporary attitudes toward violence on both continents. It is tempting to romanticise Africa by forgetting that slavery and human sacrifice preceded European encroachment or presenting the few chiefs who resisted as paragons of altruism. However, this would be a misrepresentation.

Having said that, it was the Europeans who initiated and oversaw these transactions, and it was they who established the parameters of what was acceptable. The men involved showed such callous disregard for human life that ex-slave Olaudah Equiano, turning the popular stereotype of African barbarism on its head, remarked: 'I was now persuaded that I had gotten into a world of bad spirits, and that they were going to kill me . . . the white people looked and acted, as I thought, in so savage a manner; for I had never seen among any people such instances of brutal cruelty.'[34]

Negroes in the Bilge, 1835 engraving of painting by German artist Johann Moritz Rugendas (Alamy)

2

A World of Bad Spirits:
Surviving the Middle Passage

*Such were the horrors of my views and fears at [that]
moment that, if ten thousand worlds had been my own, I
would have freely parted with them all to have exchanged
my condition with that of the meanest slave in my own
country.*[1]

Olaudah Equiano (ex-slave), 1789

It is easy to regard those Africans who experienced the
middle passage as passive victims trapped in a dark, unend-
ing nightmare, but to do so would be to ignore a weight of
evidence to the contrary. Although terrified and debilitated,
many found ways to fight back, risking life and limb in the
attempt. The odds were hugely stacked against them yet they
refused to accept their fate. While ships' captains commonly
under-reported events and conditions during voyages, particularly incidents of escape or rebellion. Around 485 records
of slave revolt have survived, suggesting that at least one in

ten voyages experienced some form of on-board mutiny or rebellion at a rate of one or two a year. Given the circumstances, these figures are nothing short of staggering.[2]

The risk of revolt was ever present. Why else would crews have gone to such lengths to prevent escape and quash any thoughts of retaliation as soon as their captives had been herded on board? Loaded muskets, nets, shackles, chains and other restraints were routine equipment, and for good reason. The crews were hugely outnumbered. After stripping the men naked, a prudent captain would have them immediately handcuffed in twos and clapped in leg irons, although women and children, perceived to be less of a threat, were often left unshackled. It was a mistake some captains lived to regret. With their greater mobility, the women had opportunities to observe not only the crew's movements but also the location of their weapons. As such, they were in an ideal position to plan, urge or help instigate revolt.

A rebellion on the *Robert* of Bristol depended on the involvement of one such female captive, who

being more at large, was to watch for the proper opportunity. She brought [Tomba, the ringleader] word one night that there were no more than five white men upon the deck, and they asleep, bringing him a hammer at the same time [all the weapons that she could find] to execute the treachery. He encouraged the accomplices what he could . . . but could now . . . engage only one more and the woman to follow him up on deck.[3]

Unfortunately for them, after dispatching two members of the crew, the rebels were overwhelmed. Three of their 'abettors' were forced to eat the heart and liver of one of their comrades before they were executed. Unlike Tomba, the woman remains nameless, yet her fate was no less cruel on account of her gender. The captain 'hoisted [her] up by the thumbs, [and] whipped and slashed her with knives, before the other slaves, till she died'.[4]

The involvement of courageous women is implicit in several accounts of successful and abortive mutinies, including desperate attempts to escape or prevent loaded ships from leaving. Ignorant of their destination and fearful of being eaten alive or brutally slain, captured Africans – mostly described in ships logs as 'the Negroes', as if to suggest they were genderless – would have known that on-board revolt had a greater chance of success when it took place in sight of land.

Somehow, they managed to overcome language barriers, sickness, cumbersome shackles and constant scrutiny to plot and make their move. They succeeded in 1704, shortly before the *Eagle* set sail from the Gold Coast, when its skeleton guard was overwhelmed, allowing 400 men, women and children to escape.[5] They succeeded again in June 1730, when ninety-six Africans, sixty-one of whom were women, subdued the crew of the *Little George* off the Guinea coast and took control of the ship. Its captain, George Scott, survived to give an account of what transpired:

On the sixth of said month at half an hour past the Clock in the Morning, being about 100 leagues distant from the Land, the Men Slaves got off their Irons and making way thro' the bulkhead of the Deck, killed the Watch consisting of John Harris (Doctor) Jonathan

Ebens (Cooper) and Thomas Ham (Sailor) who were
thought all asleep. I being then in my Cabin and hearing
Noise upon Deck (they throwing the Watch overboard)
took my Pistol directly, and fired up the Scuttle
which . . . made all the Slaves that were loose run
forwards except for one or two men who seemed to laugh
at the Cowardice of the rest, and in defiance of us, being
but four Men and a Boy . . . kept us confined in the
Cabin.[6]

These desperate, outraged people managed to sail the ship
back to the mouth of the Sierra Leone river, where an intel-
ligent deal was struck: the lives of the surviving crew would
be spared in exchange for the African people's freedom.
Having made it ashore with no further bloodshed, the men
and women abandoned ship, leaving the crew to their fate.

Not all ships' crews were as fortunate. Two years later, off
the coast of Guinea, Captain John Major was killed along
with his entire crew when his ship was 'seized upon by the
Negroes'.[7] Ten years later, in 1742, while taking on slaves in
the Sierra Leone river, the captain of the *Jolly Batchelor* and
two members of his crew were attacked and killed with the
help of a group of Africans on shore. Guerrilla style, they
freed their fellow captives in the hold, stripped the vessel of
its rigging and sails and rapidly abandoned ship.[8] The same
fate befell the crew of the *Nancy* in 1767, at the mouth of
the Bonny River, when a group of over 200 men and women
overpowered them.[9] There are many more such accounts.

Although the chances of success were much reduced once
ships had set sail, revolt was even attempted en route to or
on arrival in the West Indies. In 1785, a British ship

reported rescuing fifteen emaciated Africans adrift on the high seas 'in a very wretched condition'. Having slain the captain and crew, they had attempted to sail the ship back to their homeland. Imagine their distress, having come so close to freedom, at being carried on to Bristol. Unfortunately, no record survives of how many men and women were in the group or what became of them.

A similar mutiny took place on the *Thomas* in 1797, shortly before the ship docked in Barbados. Again, women are cited as the instigators. Temporarily released from their confinement to take exercise and refreshment on deck, they armed themselves with the contents of an unlocked musket chest, overwhelmed the crew, released the shackled men and helped take control of the ship. With no knowledge of how to navigate, they ended up drifting for six weeks until a British warship attacked and subdued them. The survivors were taken on to Cape Nicola Mole in Haiti, where they were sold.[10]

On arrival in the Americas, surviving a rebellion depended on being close enough to navigate, wade to or swim ashore. In modern-day Ecuador, the province of Esmereldas is said to be populated by the descendants of a shipload of mutinous slaves who escaped when their ship became stranded en route from Panama to Lima in 1553. Whether women were among them is unknown, but the Maroon settlements they established would become a safe haven for other escapees in future years. The population of Esmereldas remains predominantly black.

On-board insurrections occurred, on average, once or twice a year throughout the slave trade period. How anyone found the energy to fight back remains a mystery. The intolerable heat, the reek of 'noxious effluvia', the inadequate diet and the chronic lack of movement meant that within days of leaving port, most of the captives in the hold were probably too debilitated to stand. Gangrene, scurvy and dysentery (known as the 'bloody flux') were rife; epidemics of small-pox or yellow fever could deplete entire shiploads, including the crew. 'Tight-packing' meant being packed like spoons on shelves less than three feet apart, with barely room to move or breathe. If they did not die from suffocation or crushing due to overcrowding, the captives risked severe dehydration in temperatures of over 100 degrees Fahrenheit. Travelling on a slave ship, whether as captive, passenger or crew, required a strong stomach. The telltale stench of a slave ship could be detected long before it came into view.

Giving evidence to a parliamentary inquiry into con-ditions on the slave ships, James Morley, who had served as both a cabin boy and a gunner, described how 'under great difficulty of breathing, the women, particularly, often got upon the beams . . . to give air'. The same inquiry heard the ship's surgeon, Alexander Falconbridge, describe how '[the Africans] are frequently stowed so close, as to admit of no other position than lying on their sides'. He recalled a 'Leverpool [sic] ship' in which 'the slaves were so crowded that they were obliged to lie one upon the other', resulting in the death of nearly half of the 600 souls on board.

Falconbridge's graphic account of the conditions he encountered below deck conjures a hellish scene:

In each of the apartments are placed three or four large buckets, of a conical form . . . to which, when necessary, the Negroes have recourse. It often happens that those who are placed at a distance from the buckets, in endeavouring to get to them, rumble over their companions in consequence of their being shackled. These accidents, although unavoidable, are productive of continuous quarrels in which some of them are always bruised. In this distressed situation, unable to proceed and prevented from getting to the tubs, they desist from the attempt; and as the necessities of nature are not to be resisted, ease themselves as they lie. This becomes a fresh source of boils and disturbances and tends to render the conditions of the poor captive wretches still more uncomfortable . . . Upon refusing to take sustenance, I have seen coals of fire, glowing hot, put on a shovel and placed so near the lips as to scorch and burn them. And this has been accompanied with threats of forcing them to swallow the coals if they persisted in refusing to eat . . . The hardships and inconveniences suffered by the Negroes during the passage are scarcely to be enumerated or conceived. They are far more violently affected by seasickness than Europeans. It frequently terminates in death, especially among the women . . . But the exclusion of fresh air is among the most intolerable . . . I was frequently witness to the fatal effects.[11]

The journey itself was interminable. For much of the seventeenth century, crossing the Atlantic from the west coast of Africa could take as long as 133 days – up to four and a half months of unrelenting misery for everyone on board. Storms were an ever-present danger and when abandoning ship, crew members rarely stopped to open up the hatches to release their terrified charges. The risks of piracy or running out of food and water were considerable, too, sometimes causing whole cargoes of slaves to be jettisoned.

In 1781, the case of the infamous *Zong* exposed such practices when the ship became the subject of a lawsuit. It only became public knowledge because the owners tried to claim on their insurance for the loss of a third of their 'cargo', following the deliberate drowning of 132 slaves when water supplies ran low. According to one eyewitness, the first batch consisted of fifty-four women and children, thrown 'singly through the cabin windows' into the sea like jetsam.[12] The terror and despair of these women as they awaited their fate, some with babies in their arms, is beyond imagining.

The *Zong*'s casualties were the victims of poor navigation, which left the ship hopelessly off course. Even uneventful crossings could last two to three months, subject to the weather, the condition of the boat and the navigational skills of the crew.[13] Captives loaded early, before the ship had purchased its full contingent, often endured several months on board in addition to the crossing time. By the early nineteenth century, improved navigation and faster, better-equipped ships had reduced the average crossing time to fifty-one days.[14] This would have been of little comfort to those who survived the journey or to the millions who perished en route.

Abnormally high mortality rates both before and after embarkation, and the tendency of ship's captains to under-report how many they threw (dead or alive) into the sea for fear of being held financially liable, have meant that estimates of the number of Africans captured for transportation are unusually broad. They range from a conservative 6 million to an emotive 100 million over 400 years. Although there is no real way of knowing how many people died before embarkation, more recent estimates of 'slaves accounted for' place the global figure at between 10 and 12 million. Three out of ten Africans are believed to have died during the crossing. At least one in every three would have been a woman.[15]

Women were twice as likely to survive the crossing as men, but this was not due to any concessions. If the shock of the experience had not stopped their periods, they lay in their menstrual blood. If pregnant, they gave birth without assistance, often to have their newborn tossed to the sharks. To add to these nightmarish conditions, and as a perk to the crew, female captives were also systematically raped. Ship surgeon James Arnold claimed that it was common practice for the captain of the *Ruby* 'on receipt of a woman slave – especially a young one – to send for her to come to his cabin so he might lie with her'.[16] Similarly, James Hawkins described how, on boarding, 'the officers had all provided themselves with three or four wives each' as a matter of course.[17] Describing these women as 'wives' was a nicety. As freed slave Ottobah Cugoano attested, 'it was common for the dirty filthy sailors to take the African women and lie upon their bodies'.[18] This may also account for the fact that so many women were found to be in the early stages of pregnancy on arrival, despite their separation from the men.

John Newton, the reformed slave trader who penned the song *Amazing Grace*, described how women and girls were 'often exposed to the rudeness of white savages'.[19] In 1753, when he was captain of the *African*, he had one of his crew placed in irons when he 'seduced a woman slave . . . and lay with her brute-like in view of the whole quarter deck'. On most ships, punishment for such excesses was rare. In the absence of a sympathetic captain, the women had to fend for themselves. Ships' surgeons and other eyewitnesses make several references to defiant women who resisted sexual assault, sometimes at the cost of their own lives.

Keen to expose the depravity of these 'dealers in human flesh', abolitionists immortalised one such assault in the form of a scathing cartoon. It refers to the trial (and subsequent acquittal due to lack of evidence) of Captain John Kimber, accused of torturing and murdering a young girl of fifteen when he was master of the *Recovery*. The girl, having resisted his attack on her 'virgin modesty', is seen being strung up by her left foot with a rope attached to a pulley. Hanging upside down, she is naked but for a small strip of cloth around her hips, an ironic concession to European sensibilities. Captain Kimber is depicted clutching his chest and laughing demonically, with a cat-o'-nine-tales at his feet. Three other women can be seen crouching in the background, as if to suggest it's their turn next. But it is the comments of the crew that are most revealing. 'My eyes, Jack', says one, 'our girls in Wapping are never flogged for their modesty' – a direct reference to the double standards that prevailed. Another sailor declares that he is 'sick of this Black Business', while the man holding one end of the rope is saying 'Damn me if I like it. I have a good mind to let go'. The cartoon suggests that crew members were largely opposed to such harsh treatment of women. In reality, with no financial stake in the venture, most could abuse their captives at will with total impunity. Access to African women's bodies was one of the few available perks for men whose chances of perishing during the crossing were almost as high as that of their captives.[20]

Crew members, many of them reluctant recruits themselves, died almost as frequently as their charges, a consequence of poor diet, contagious diseases, excessive punishments and frequent accidents. As late as the 1780s, 20 per cent of all crew members are thought to have perished on slave ships out of Bristol and Liverpool. Many would have fallen victim to the excesses of overzealous officers who were ever alert to the risk of insubordination or mutiny.[21] Captain Rice Harris, a slaver from Bristol, was sent to the gallows for murdering a member of his crew 'in circumstances of horrible barbarity'. He was one of several notoriously sadistic commanders – which included men like Captain James Newton, who was sentenced to hang for the murder of his wife and several members of his crew. A popular ditty among sailors in those times speaks volumes: 'Beware and take care of the Bight of Benin', they sang, 'for one that comes out, there are forty go in'.

Given the confines below deck, opportunities for physical exercise on deck, subject to good weather, presented a rare opportunity for on-board insurrection. Forced to 'dance' – a euphemism for jumping on deadened, suppurating limbs to the accompaniment of a drum or occasionally a violin or a flute – captives risked a severe flogging if they refused. A diary entry by Reverend John Riland, who travelled out of Liverpool on a slave ship to Jamaica in 1801, observed that on such occasions, the women 'kept themselves aloof . . . and seemed to feel an indignation which long continued habit could not suppress when forced to behave foolishly'. Some women preferred to throw themselves overboard rather than suffer such humiliation. Riland goes on to describe how a woman who made a failed attempt to drown herself was handcuffed and mercilessly punished.[22] Little wonder that when forced to sing, the captives could only find it in themselves to voice 'melancholy lamentations'.

To subdue all thoughts of resistance, floggings were frequent and arbitrary, as were various methods of torture. In keeping with the times, some ships' officers thought nothing of applying neck irons or thumbscrews as a warning to others. Sir Thomas Phillips, master of the *Hannibal,* reported in 1694 that it was common practice to 'cut off the legs and arms of the most wilful to terrify the rest'.[23] Despite such threats, Africans' refusal to submit remained a major headache for their captors.

One of their greatest fears was the risk of attempted suicide, including defiant acts of mass suicide. This same Captain Phillips noted that 'the Negroes are so wilful and loath to leave their own country that they have often leap'd out of the canoes, boat or ship into the sea, and kept under water until they were drowned'. With a mortality rate of 43 per cent on the ensuing voyage, those who perished in this way may have been among the lucky few. Just over forty years later, in 1736, 100 slaves are reported to have jumped together into the Atlantic Ocean from the deck of the *Prince of Orange.* Although the crew attempted to retrieve them, thirty-three succeeded in drowning themselves.[24] Two women were among those who died after leaping from an American ship off the coast of Accra in 1776.[25] Ten of the Africans who perished on the *Zong* preferred to jump than be pushed. And the list goes on.

A widespread belief that death would reunite the captives with their ancestors suggests that suicide was seen not just as an act of resistance but as a longed-for release. Sir Hans Sloane, writing of his travels to the West Indies in 1701, remarked that some Africans, 'imagining they shall change their condition . . . from servile to free, cut their throats'.[26] A century later, French traveller Jaques Savary suggested homesickness was a factor when he remarked that

> from the moment that the slaves are embarked, one must put the sails up. The reason is that these slaves have so great a love for their country that they despair when they see that they are leaving it forever; that makes them die of grief, and I have heard merchants . . . say that they died more often before leaving the port than during the voyage. Some drown themselves into the sea, others hit their head against the ship, others hold their breath and try to smother themselves, others still try to die of hunger from not eating.[27]

Attempts at voluntary starvation were so common that many ships carried a 'speculum oris', a gruesome, scissor-like instrument with serrated blades that was pushed between the teeth of captives who had lost the will to eat. Operated by means of a hefty thumbscrew, the blades winched the victim's jaws apart, allowing food to be forced down their throat. But more often than not, suicide involved succumbing to a 'fixed melancholy'. With no choice but to lie in their own filth, captives quickly became depressed or unhinged. Guinea surgeon Matthew Morley, whose role was to protect the interests of investors by keeping as many slaves as possible alive, refers to several women who refused to eat or died of 'lethargy' or 'sulkiness'. Their suicide was clearly a conscious and wilful act, despite being prompted by mounting despair.[28]

Olaudah Equiano, whose account must speak for the millions who were silenced, describes how 'the shrieks of women and the groans of the dying rendered the whole scene of horror inconceivable'. Once exposed to the conditions below deck, it was not long before he too became 'so sick and low that I was not able to eat, nor had I the least desire to taste anything. I now wished for the last friend, death, to relieve me.'[29]

So, who stood to benefit from all this needless suffering? The Royal African Company (previously the Royal Adventurers) first monopolised the trade for Britain, with the full and eager backing of the English monarchy. Granted a 1,000-year monopoly by royal charter in 1660, it appointed the king's brother as its president and relied on its wealthy patrons for funds. Investors and shareholders included at least four members of the royal family, two dukes, a marquess, five earls, four barons and seven knights. Philosopher John Locke was a subscriber; even Samuel Pepys, the popular diarist, had a share.[30]

Their monopoly was short-lived. In 1698, an act of Parliament opened the floodgates for individual traders, known as the ten percenters. Henceforth, any Tom, Dick or Harry who could afford the cost of leasing a ship plus the 10 per cent duty paid on goods exported during the first leg of the journey was at liberty to take part. But there were others who wanted a slice of the pie. Half a century later, the Company of Merchants, an alliance of London, Bristol and Liverpool traders, was formed, making it 'lawful for all his Majesty's Subjects to trade and traffick to and from any Port or Place in Africa, between the Port of Sallee in South Barbary and the Cape of Good Hope, when and at such Times, and in such Manner; and in or with such Quantity of Goods, Wares or Merchandises, as he or they shall think fit'.

Potential losses on the middle passage may have been high, but the profits to be made were huge and self-generating. Some merchants are known to have factored in an attrition rate of between 30 and 50 per cent and still made a fortune. A typical triangular voyage involved the exchange of goods exported from Britain in return for captured Africans. Proceeds from their sale in the Americas were then used to purchase sugar, rum, cotton, tobacco, coffee, spices and other local produce for resale in Europe. Britons took full advantage of the many opportunities to get rich quick. Indeed, the nation's rise to world dominance could not have occurred without the unprecedented wealth generated by the sale of African slaves and the blatant exploitation of their labour.

Profits weren't just about the trade in human lives. Shipbuilding flourished and whole industries arose to service Britain's young colonies, including a thriving transportation system for carrying people and goods to the so-called New World. Propaganda and press gangs lured around 300,000 white indentured labourers to Britain's tobacco colonies during the seventeenth century. Despite high mortality rates caused by the conditions on board ship and the diseases they encountered, this steady migration continued, either to Britain's mainland American colonies of Virginia and Maryland or to the West Indies, ensuring that the wealthy could both establish new plantations and manage the growing population of slaves who would eventually replace these white labourers. Writing in 1668, Sir Josiah Child claimed that 'one Englishman, with the Blacks that work with him, accounting what they eat, use and wear, would make employment for four men back in England'. Britain's economy flourished. By the end of the seventeenth century, the African trade and its various offshoots accounted for around 36 per cent of Britain's commercial profits.[31]

Bristol's population grew by over 40,000 in the span of a century, transforming it into 'a city of shopkeepers'. Between 1698 and 1807, Bristol's merchants financed over 2,000 voyages, transporting over half a million enslaved Africans to the Americas. Having overtaken London in the 1730s, its citizens gained such a well-earned reputation for being 'driven by trade' that it was later said of the city that there was 'not one brick that has not been cemented with the blood of slaves'. Even its clergy were said to 'talk of nothing but trade and how to turn a penny'.[32] The scale of involvement was so great that, in today's money, Bristol's citizens were awarded over £2 million in compensation when the 1833 Slave Emancipation Act finally came into force in August 1834. Needless to say, not a single penny was paid to the people they had enslaved.

One of the unforeseen consequences of this involvement was a growing black presence in Britain. For eminent merchants with West Indian connections, many of whom had been ships' captains before they invested their profits in commerce, the appendage of an African slave was seen as a status symbol. Their wives and daughters would parade black children around like poodles, treating them as little more than pets. Advertisements seeking to appoint a new black servant or appealing for the capture of an old one became commonplace in Bristol's newspapers. Reading between the lines, it is clear that some of these black servants were articulate, highly skilled and far from content with their lot. One such advertisement, for example, calls for the return of 'a healthy Negro girl, aged about fifteen years, (who) speaks good English, works at her needle, washes well, does household work and has had the smallpox'.[33]

The names of the women and girls who serviced these rich Bristolians are mostly unknown, but local graveyards and church records confirm their visible presence, describing them as 'Negroes' or 'blacks'. They include Joan Smyth, buried in 1603; Ann Jones, baptised in Temple Church in 1704; Venus, married to a slave called Commodore in St Michaels Church in 1721; Catherine Smith, buried in St Stephens Church in 1724; Rebecca Rice, married in the church of St Augustine the Less in September 1728 to William (also black); their daughters Mary, Betty and Susannah; and Philis Quaco, who was buried in the same church in 1740.[34]

By the 1730s, the average voyage out of Bristol harbour, purchasing 170 slaves en route, was making a profit of £8,000, a small fortune by today's standards. In 1753, twenty of Britain's 120 sugar refineries were based there, owned by some of its most prominent citizens. For those with sufficient capital, there were huge fortunes to be made. By 1769, James Laroche, reputedly Bristol's most prolific merchant trader, had backed no less than 132 voyages in just over forty years. Like many of his kind, he went on to become an MP, throwing his weight behind the campaign for free trade in slaves. Other wealthy merchants and slave owners followed in his footsteps, defending their vested interests by doing everything in their power to thwart abolitionist demands when they began lobbying for change.

Liverpool experienced a similar boom. Previously little more than a fishing village, its population swelled from 5,000 in 1700 to 78,000 by the end of the century. By 1750, it was sending more ships to Africa than London and Bristol combined, so that by 1783, the city's annual profits amounted to £300,000. Its strategic location made for easy contact with suppliers in other parts of the country, and its merchants grew fat on the proceeds. By 1807, when the act to abolish the trade was finally passed, Liverpool was responsible for 80 per cent of British voyages and the transport of 1.5 million Africans. Known as 'the capital of the slave trade', its streets were said to be 'marked out by chains'.[35]

In towns and cities across the country, wealthy men scrambled for a piece of the action. Lyme Regis, Poole, Dorset, Exeter, Topsham, Plymouth, Lancaster, Berwick, Weymouth, Falmouth, Dartmouth, Portsmouth, Deal and Whitehaven all had a stake in the African trade, expanding or growing rich as a direct or indirect result of the traffic in slaves. West Indian colonies needed a constant supply of imported goods to maintain both planters and labourers. Local industry rose to the challenge.

British exports included clothing, textiles and wool for blankets from Manchester and other Lancashire towns; guns, iron bars, nails, chains and restraints from Birmingham; copper and brass from Warrington, Wigan and Holywell; and customised coarse blue stockings from Leicester. Other parts of the country supplied sailcloth and rope; beds, chairs and stools; brass, pewter and copper pots; cooking implements; sugar stoves; iron rollers; beer, cider, wine and spirits; glass beads; and a variety of durable foodstuffs. Meanwhile, financial institutions like Lloyds of London made sure that ships' cargoes were insured against unforeseen losses, including the death of transported slaves.

The trade in African lives proved so beneficial that parliamentary petitions by abolitionists in 1774, 1776 and 1783 were effectively laughed out of court. But as ordinary British people and 'polite society' became acquainted with the realities of the Guinea trade, the momentum to abolish it grew. In 1788, over 100 petitions were presented to the British Parliament. Hannah Moore, an influential playwright, wrote the anti-slavery poem *Slavery*[36] to coincide with the first parliamentary debate on the subject. 'Whene'er to Afric's shores I turn my eyes', she wrote, 'Horrors of deepest, deadliest guilt arise' – an expression of the mounting national conscience that fuelled the abolitionists' campaign.

Hannah Moore was one of several women abolitionists who lent their voices to the growing outcry against the trade. They include Ann Yearsley, Maria and Harriet Falconar, Anna Letitia Barbauld, Martha Gurney, Mary Morris Knowles, Harriet Martineau and Mary Birkett Card, whose 1792 publication *A Poem on the African Slave Trade, Addressed to her own Sex – in Two Parts,* persuaded a growing number of women to boycott West Indian sugar.[37] Written when she was just seventeen years old, her poem appeals to her fellow 'sisters' to recognise their own contribution to the suffering of enslaved Africans, calling on them to abstain from using sugar and other goods produced by slaves. She also suggests they use their feminine powers to persuade their menfolk to follow suit.

Thanks to such interventions, by 1792 the number of parliamentary petitions had grown to 519, with over 400,000 names demanding an end to the trade. These protests were effectively ignored for another fifteen years. Like carbon-emitting industries today, the African trade was seen as an unfortunate but necessary evil. The luxuries it generated were hard to give up, even though people were aware of the consequences. As one anonymous poet put it:

> I own I am shock'd at the purchase of slaves,
> And fear those who buy them and sell them are
>   knaves,
> What I hear of their hardships, their tortures and
>   groans,
> Is almost enough to drive pity from stones,
> I pity them greatly, but I must be mum,
> For how could we do without sugar and rum?
> Especially sugar, so needful we see
> What, give up our dessert, our coffee and tea?[38]

The abolitionists had a long fight ahead of them against a formidable opponent. Composed of wealthy slave owners and merchant traders, the West India lobby was extremely powerful and defended its members' interests to the last.

The price of their recalcitrance was the lives of millions of Africans. As the ships that these men had financed and equipped limped into some distant port, firing their guns to announce their arrival and the completion of the second leg of their journey, the profits from such ventures were virtually guaranteed.

The crew knew exactly what to do, for their wages depended on it. Bodies were doused with sea water, skin was oiled and leaky bowels plugged with a cork. Once assembled on deck, their debilitated captives were inspected and divided into lots for sale to the highest bidder. With the degradations of the voyage behind them, these bewildered Africans might have hoped that the worst of their suffering was over. But the rough handling of buyers who flocked to the dockside slave markets can only have increased their apprehension. Breasts were squeezed, jaws prized apart, and genitals prodded and poked as the fittest amongst them were selected for auction. Olaudah's experience would have been typical:

At last we came in sight of the Island of Barbados, at which the whites on board gave a great shout and made many signs of joy to us . . . Many merchants and planters came on board, though it was evening. They put us in separate parcels and examined us attentively. They also made us jump, and pointed to the land, signifying that we were to go there. We thought by this that we should be eaten by these ugly men, as they appeared to us . . . They told us we were not to be eaten but to work, and were soon to go on land where we should see many of our country people . . . We were conducted immediately to the merchant's yard, where we were all pent up together like so many sheep in a fold without regard to sex or age.[39]

They had clung to life against all odds. Yet even in their wildest dreams, nothing could have prepared them for what lay ahead, as they began their onward journey to life on a West Indian plantation. For the survivors, men and women alike, the nightmare had only just begun.

Sugar cane cutters, Jamaica, circa 1890 (Caribbean Photo Archive)

3

Labour Pains:
Enslaved Women and Production

A Negro man is purchased either for a trade or the culti-
vation of the different processes of the cane [but] the
occupations of women are only two, the house with its
several departments and supposed indulgencies, or the field
with its exaggerated labours.

> William Beckford, *Remarks Upon the Situation*
> *of Negroes in Jamaica* (London, 1788)

What was the fate of the African women who survived that horrendous journey across the Atlantic? And how did the skills, knowledge and intuitions they carried with them naked to the Americas enable them not only to survive the daily trials of plantation slavery, but also to resist and fight back? This account of systematic, gendered brutality does not make easy reading, but after centuries of historical amnesia, these questions deserve an answer. They can only be addressed by looking at what enslaved women had to contend with, for it is in the detail of their experience that we will begin to appreciate their phenomenal spirit of survival.

Jamaica has to be one of the best places to start. The island not only experienced as many slave rebellions as all the other British West Indian colonies combined, it was also famous for its Maroons – women and men, many of them born in Africa, who preferred self-determination to enslavement and were prepared to fight to the death to defend it. Maroons like Nanny and her brothers plagued the European planters from the earliest period of Spanish settlement at the start of the sixteenth century until the second Maroon treaty was signed with the British in 1760. Their militant legacy survives in Jamaica to this day, as does Nanny's grave.[1]

Several factors made the situation in Jamaica unique. Twenty-six times bigger than Barbados, it was by far the largest of Britain's West Indian colonies. Both its climate and its terrain were ideal for large-scale sugar production, requiring a labour force of tens of thousands. As long as imported Africans could be forced to work, there were huge fortunes to be made. But from a European standpoint, there was one major hitch. The high demand for imported Africans meant that the planters and their agents would soon find themselves hopelessly outnumbered.

The enslaved population in Jamaica grew to such an extent that by 1800, there was a ratio of twelve slaves to every white settler. In practice, this meant that relations between masters and their workforce were underpinned by the constant dread of retaliation, generating a climate of fear among the white population that, at times, bordered on hysteria. Added to its size and geography, this racial imbalance in the island's population made for a turbulent history of rebellion.

The planters' repressive practices were meant to keep slave resistance in check, but they didn't succeed. Their cruelty backfired, fuelling the anger and resentment of those they'd enslaved. As a result, not a single decade passed without a major incident. Tacky's Rebellion of 1760, which took six months to quash, and the Christmas Rebellion of 1831 led by Sam Sharpe are the best remembered, but at least twenty-two other instances of revolt or unrest were recorded in Jamaica between 1655 and 1832.[2] Meanwhile, up in the hills, the subversive activities of the Maroons who were hell-bent on defending their autonomy must have fanned the proverbial flames. Despite an eventual treaty with the British that required them to assist in external colonial wars and the hunting of runaways, their ability to sustain their own self-reliant communities would have served as a tantalising beacon of freedom.[3]

There are several theories as to why Jamaica was so prone to revolt. Early Jamaican planters, faced with frontier conditions, are known to have expressed a preference for male slaves. Over 70 per cent of slave imports are thought to have been male prior to 1700, providing a perfect crucible for tempers fuelled by testosterone and the frustrations of stolen liberty. However, some evidence suggests that considerably more women were transported in those early years than was first thought, so this perception may be skewed.[4] There was also a growing preference on the island for Gold Coast 'Coromantees', an Akan tribe who were renowned for their courage and physical prowess. The dominance of their languages and beliefs, combined with their proven military skills, undoubtedly served as a rallying cry.[5] Whatever the reasons, a distinct culture of resistance was established in Jamaica almost from the outset.

As demand for sugar increased, enslaved people found themselves caught in a spiralling cycle of violence, retaliation and repression, aggravated by the planters' growing paranoia. Little wonder that once the colony became established, most slave owners made themselves scarce. Mindful of their personal health and safety, and craving 'polite' society, they preferred to reside in more temperate climes, where they could indulge in the less arduous pursuits of the landed gentry.

Jamaica's roll call of absentee landlords is long and impressive. William Beckford, member of Parliament and twice Lord Mayor of London, owned 22,000 acres and several estates. His resulting fortune paid for the priceless antiques at Charlecote Park in Warwickshire. There was also Richard Pennant, who used the profits from his Jamaican plantations to lavishly furnish Penrhyn Castle in Wales. Richard Watt started out at as a ship hand and ended up as the owner of Speke Hall near Liverpool. Richard Oswald, a Glaswegian, built himself a palace he named Auchincruive in Ayr. And the list goes on.[6]

By 1832, two years before slavery was officially abolished, men such as these owned 84 per cent of Jamaica's sugar estates.[7] Their descendants populate the boardrooms of some of Britain's longest-standing institutions, and no doubt many of them continue to enjoy the proceeds. Visit their stately homes, however, and hardly a word is said. The huge wealth generated by the enslavement of Africans remains one of Britain's best-kept secrets.

Because the more affluent plantation owners used their substantial profits to finance the building of ships, ports, factories, tenements and other monuments to their largesse, they are often immortalised in statues. Revered as great statesmen or philanthropists, they tend to be portrayed as charitable do-gooders who spared no expense in pursuit of their civic duties. This may well be true, but at what cost? Bristol was one of several British cities that experienced 'a riot of building'. The arts flourished, too, as the idle rich sought distraction from their pampered lifestyle. Yet for all their apparent gentility, these men were entirely dependent on the dictates of the world sugar market and the compliance of those they'd enslaved.

To maintain their wealth and status, they were prepared to sanction a form of coercive labour – part agricultural, part industrial – that was one of the most extreme and dehumanising systems ever devised. As profits dipped and soared, their dirty work fell largely to agents and overseers – unscrupulous fortune seekers for the most part, who made free use of the whip in their quest to maximise returns from exports of sugar and rum.[8]

While absentee landlords enjoyed the fruits of their ill-gotten gains back home, the people they'd stolen and enslaved were literally worked to death. Both male and female field labourers worked six days a week year-round, whatever the weather, with just two or three days off for Christmas and other religious festivals. The two-year 'seasoning' process, in which new arrivals were broken like horses, proved so relentless that during the first half of the eighteenth century, around one in three Africans perished within three years of their arrival, either from disease or overwork. Surviving plantation records may be sparse, but they tell a grim story. For example, on Jamaica's Worthy Park estate, the life expectancy of someone born into slavery is estimated to have been less than thirty years, while for newly imported Africans, it was barely twelve.[9] In other words, whether transported from Africa or island-born, they dropped like proverbial flies.

Enslaved women were typically the beasts of burden across the West Indies. Confined to the lowest, most exploited ranks, only a small minority of midwives, 'doctresses', domestic servants and housekeepers were able to escape the daily hardships of field labour. At times, in the absence of a white mistress, a housekeeper might double as a concubine and find herself elevated to a tenuous position of influence, but opportunities like this were relatively few. The vast majority of women and girls were expected to perform the more menial and monotonous tasks associated with the production of huge quantities of sugar, even if it killed them.

And kill them it did. As long as imported African labour was relatively cheap to replenish, planters could afford to use people rather than animals to perform the most back-breaking tasks. After all, slaves were dispensable, whereas horses and oxen were costlier to import and less likely to survive in the unforgiving climate. In practice, this meant that enslaved women of all ages were subjected to the same relentless work regime as the men, with few if any concessions. Whether in an advanced stage of pregnancy, early motherhood or approaching old age, they could be seen labouring in the fields from sunup to sundown. Indeed, on many estates it was the women, not the men, who performed much of the heaviest labour. On Jamaica's Mesopotamia estate, for example, surviving records confirm that by the end of the eighteenth century, as much as two-thirds of its agricultural labour force was made up of women and girls.[10]

This situation was by no means unique to Jamaica. In Barbados, the first of Britain's West Indian colonies to cultivate sugar, women outnumbered men not just in the fields but in the colony as a whole from the start of the eighteenth century. For the majority of females, field work was unavoidable, so much so that graduating from the second to the first gang was taken as a sign that a girl had reached womanhood. For example, on the Newton estate in 1776, just over 61 per cent of the slave population was comprised of females. Of the sixty-two adult women slaves, fifty-one were in the first or great gang, which contained the strongest and most resilient workers. Equally telling is the fact that just two years later, six of these women were described as 'old' or 'superannuated' – in other words, no longer able to work.[11] No wonder the island's planters considered most of their women fieldworkers to be past their figurative sell-by date by age thirty-five.

Women were destined to become the backbone of the workforce on plantations across the West Indies. Records from Worthy Park estate show that over half a century *before* the African trade was halted, seventy women but only twenty-nine men were labouring in the fields – a time when they were still importing far greater numbers of men. In Grenada, a late starter by comparison, planters were admitting that 'females compose the most numerous and effective part of the field gangs of the estate' as late as 1824 – just ten years before slavery was officially abolished.[12] A similar situation could be found in the French Antilles, where women outnumbered men in the field gangs by as many as three to one on some plantations.[13]

Ironically, once outside pressure to abolish the slave trade threatened to cut off fresh supplies from Africa, even more women seem to have ended up in the fields. This is evident from Mesopotamia's records for 1809, which list ninety-two women but only forty-five men as 'fieldworkers', with thirty-one women compared to twenty-nine men in the great gang, which performed the heaviest work. Similarly high ratios were recorded toward the end of the eighteenth century at Roaring River estate and several other large plantations in Jamaica.[14]

The million-dollar question is *why*? Traditionally regarded as the 'weaker' sex, why would women be expected to perform so much more of the hardest labour? As mentioned, one explanation is that men had access to a wider range of options. Enslaved men could be blacksmiths, carpenters, coach drivers, coopers, masons, distillers or sugar boilers, whereas for most women the only choice, if it can be called that, was between 'the house with its . . . supposed indulgencies, or the field with its exaggerated labours'.

Another possible explanation is that women field labourers were preferred because they were believed to possess greater stamina and physical endurance.[15] A typical day's work lasted twelve hours in the blazing heat, with a half-hour break for breakfast and an hour and a half for lunch. Food and water, often in short supply, were heavily rationed. The work itself was gruelling, requiring an endless round of cane-hole digging, planting, hoeing, cane cutting and hauling canes to the mills. Under such circumstances, women's stamina and endurance were probably as vital to production as men's physical strength.

Scotsman William Dickson, who was secretary to the governor of Barbados for 1783–1786, witnessed these conditions first-hand. Unlike many of his contemporaries, he soon developed a strong aversion to slavery, having seen for himself that 'the great body of the slaves, the field-people . . . are generally treated more like beasts of burden than like human creatures'.[16] A Swiss traveller, Justin Girod-Chantrans, who visited the French colony of Saint-Domingue around the same time, echoed Dickson's views. Appalled by what he saw, he recorded his observations of the great gang at work in some detail, concluding that 'there is no domestic animal from which as much work is required as slaves and to which as little care is given'.

The cane-hole digging he described involved prolonged and strenuous activity in all weather:

There were about a hundred men and women of different ages, all occupied in digging ditches in a cane-field, the majority of them naked or covered with rags. The sun shone down with full force on their heads. Sweat rolled from all parts of their bodies. Their limbs, weighed down by the heat, fatigued with the weight of their picks and by the resistance of the clayey soil baked hard enough to break their implements, strained themselves to overcome every obstacle. A mournful silence reigned. Exhaustion was stamped on every face, but the hour of rest had not come. The pitiless eye of the

manager patrolled the gang of several foremen armed
with long whips, moving periodically between them,
giving stinging blows to all who, worn out by fatigue,
were compelled to take a rest – men or women, young
or old without distinction.[17]

The realities of such an existence are hard to imagine, but
activities like the transport of manure provide a telling
glimpse. With the soil needing constant replenishment,
baskets of manure, each weighing around eighty pounds,
had to be carried on the head for distribution across
hundreds of acres of cultivated land. The distance between
the fields and the cattle pens where the dung was collected
could be as much as a mile or more over rough, uneven
ground, and on average every acre of land needed around
sixty-four tonnes of manure.[18] The toll this kind of work
would have taken on women's bodies, particularly pregnant
or nursing mothers, is inconceivable.

Even in Barbados, where planters claimed to harbour
more benign attitudes towards their women field hands,
they suffered 'every hardship which can be supposed to
attend oppressive toil'. According to Dickson, it was not
uncommon to see women 'far gone in their pregnancy,
toiling in the field' or to see 'naked infants . . . exposed to
the weather, sprawling on a goatskin or in a wooden tray'.
He grew used to hearing 'drivers curse both them and their
squalling brats, when they were suckling them'.[19] Mothers
with young babies were expected to keep up with the rest of
the gang, often with the added weight of an infant strapped
to their backs. Assuming they survived that long, they
could expect to stay in the fields for upwards of twenty

years. Their status stood in stark contrast to attitudes toward white women at the time, who were mostly seen as frail and decorative.

There was one notable exception. In the early years, particularly in Barbados, white indentured labourers (or 'white niggers' as they were also called) were often expected to work alongside the enslaved in the fields. Some indentured women had been transported to the colonies as convicts or prostitutes, others had been duped or press ganged. Whatever their story, they were afforded no special status. Diseases and physical exhaustion meant their chances of survival were slim. But by the mid-seventeenth century, slavery and skin colour had become permanently linked in European minds. Before long, white women were effectively barred from field labour on account of their more 'delicate' constitution. However lowly their origins, however desperate their circumstances, their status as 'misses' was assured, leaving black women, paupers and princesses alike, firmly at the bottom of the pecking order.[20]

Among the planter class, most white women showed precious little sympathy for their black and brown sisters slaving away in the fields. Their loyalties lay firmly with their menfolk, with colour as the great divider. Outside of Barbados, white women were relatively few in number, but their attitude is typified in the comments of Janet Shaw, a Scottish 'Lady of Quality', who accompanied her brother on a visit to Antigua and St Kitts in 1774. Although she thought of herself as humane, she had no difficulty buying into the prevailing view of Africans as 'brutes', describing them as immune to physical suffering and 'perfectly indifferent to their fate'. Having observed the conditions of the

field gangs over a period of months, she can almost be seen
shrugging her shoulders. 'When one comes to be better
acquainted with the nature of the Negroes', she remarked,
'the horrour [sic] of it must wear off.'[21]

Across the West Indies, generations of black women and
girls toiled and sweated. For them, the 'horrour' that Janet
Shaw referred to was nothing short of an inherited life
sentence, as daughters followed their mothers and grandmothers into the cane fields. Even for small children,
conditions were unimaginably harsh. Put to work almost as
soon as they could walk, they were usually supervised by an
elderly female slave, who taught them to pull weeds, pick
off insects, carry water to the fields and perform other
duties suited to their age. As they grew older, they would
graduate to the third, second and first gangs, performing
more and more arduous tasks.

This early enslavement of children was both physical and
mental. Conditioned from a young age into accepting their
lot as normal and somehow deserved, they would have
known no other reality. Unless someone told them differently – their mother, perhaps, or the old African woman
who looked after them – they were destined to grow up
believing the myth that black people were condemned by
God into perpetual servitude because of the colour of
their skin.

As the number of island-born slaves increased, somehow
women's life expectancy improved. Consequently, planters
and agents across the Caribbean began to view women
fieldworkers as an increasingly attractive prospect. They
measured their slaves' worth solely in terms of productivity

and they were quick to do the math. If a minority of the workforce performed proportionately more of the hard labour *and* survived significantly longer, they were clearly a more profitable investment. Their financial calculations and forecasts certainly reflect this kind of reasoning. Given the relentless quest for profit that drove the plantation economy, the implications are obvious: as far as planters were concerned, black women's labour was of equal value to black men's, sometimes more.

Nowhere is this more apparent than in their selling price. In Barbados, as early as 1673, the cost of a female slave was just under £21 while the price of a male was just under £19. Bajan planters were among the first to recognise that potential mothers represented a higher return on their investment, so despite fluctuations over the next fifty years, the difference in price remained paltry.[22] A relatively small differential was the norm on other islands too. For example, in Jamaica, toward the end of the eighteenth century, a male slave could be purchased for between £50 and £70, while the price of a healthy female was £50 to £60.[23] Around the same time in Grenada, where men outnumbered women by five to three, a Creole man was valued at £60 and a woman at £50.[24]

Predictably, as the prospect of abolition loomed, these prices trebled. By 1803, the highest-calibre slaves both male and female could fetch as much as £160 in Barbados. Similarly, on Grenada's Pearl estate, in a detailed inventory of the property, male and female slaves were valued at £180 and £170 respectively.[25] Since it was their age, skills and physical condition that determined how much they could fetch, it is just as telling that a ten-year-old girl and a

twelve-year-old boy were valued in the same inventory at
£140 each, suggesting that their potential as future labourers was thought to be equal. Even a fifty-year-old woman
approaching the end of her working life was expected to
fetch £150. The evidence may be patchy, but it cries out for
a reassessment of the popular stereotype (inspired and
favoured by the planters themselves) that men were the
most valuable assets in the slave force.

It is no coincidence that this idea had such an appeal at
the time. By the end of the eighteenth century, with opposition to slavery gathering momentum back in Britain, it was
very much in the planters' interests to play down the number
of women who worked in the fields. Their treatment of
enslaved women had become a bone of contention, and
members of the West Indies lobby were keen to defend their
interests by highlighting efforts to improve their conditions.
The growing boycott of West Indian sugar, spearheaded by
abolitionist women, had begun to take effect. Faced with
mounting criticism and the prospect of falling sugar prices,
planters were probably not averse to massaging the figures to
project themselves in a better light.[26]

Deliberate or not, this tendency to undervalue women's
contribution proved remarkably persuasive. When a parliamentary committee on the slave trade took evidence in
1791, planters and their advocates presented a suspiciously
rosy picture of plantation life. When they couldn't defend
their practices, they blamed the victims, arguing that the
slaves were suited to their condition and did not aspire to
freedom. But as Mary Prince put it so eloquently, 'they put
a cloak about the truth. It is not so. All slaves want to be
free – to be free is very sweet.'[27]

Of course, the popular image of gangs of slaves hard at work in the fields only tells part of the story. In reality, sugar production required a highly organised workforce to run the mills and boiling houses that sprang into action during the cropping season. The pressure to produce endless hogsheads of sugar would have dominated every waking moment. To keep the mills running, slaves often laboured through the night, working alternate shifts of twelve and eighteen hours for up to six months of the year. Since the more skilled occupations in the mill-house were reserved for men, women were confined to the drudgery, risking life and limb as they fed the huge rollers with cane or tended the boiling vats of cane juice.

Transforming harvested cane into crystallised sugar was a skilled and precarious activity involving the extraction of cane juice and a slow heating process. Vertical, three-roller mills, powered by wind, water or animals, were used across the Caribbean, and with labour in such ready supply, there was little incentive for planters to improve the technology. Water-driven mills, thought to be faster and more efficient, were particularly hazardous since they needed to be constantly fed. Overtiredness and a general disregard for safety made the problem even worse. Frenchman Jean-Baptiste (Père) Labat, a proprietor of the Fond Saint Jaques estate in Martinique, described the consequences for women millworkers in chilling detail. Writing at the start of the eighteenth century, he observed that

> accidents were frequent among female slaves . . . particu-
> larly at night when, exhausted by hard labour during the
> daytime, they fall asleep while passing the canes

[through the rollers]. Dragged towards the machinery which they follow involuntarily still clutching the canes in their hands, they thus become caught up in it and crushed before they can be rescued. This is particularly the case when the mill is water-driven where the movement is so rapid that it is physically impossible to stop it in time to save the lives of those whose fingers are already drawn in. On such occasions, the quickest remedy is to promptly sever the arm with a bill (which is why it makes sense to keep one . . . sharp and ready to use if needed). It is better to cut off the arm than to see a person passing through the rollers of the mill. This precaution has been very useful to us at Fond S(aint) Jaques where one of our women slaves was drawn into the mill. Fortunately for her . . . a male slave was able to stop the mill in time to give us the opportunity to sever half of the mangled arm, and thus save the rest of her body. A woman slave belonging to the Jesuits was not as fortunate. In attempting to pass something to the woman on the other side of the mill, her shirt sleeves became caught in the cogs, and her arm, followed by the rest of her body was drawn into the machinery in an instant, before she could be given help. Only the head does not pass; it separates from the neck and falls on the side where the body entered.

Labat was an ordained priest, yet there's not a hint of sentimentality in his description of these gruesome events. In a context where it took just eighteen months to recoup the cost of a slave, profit was king. Like other Europeans who benefited from the regime, this man of the cloth shrugged off the suffering he witnessed, arguing that, casualties or not, it was 'absolutely necessary' to have slaves.[28]

Back in Europe, politicians were fully aware of the toll on women's bodies. Giving evidence to a parliamentary inquiry into slavery, William Taylor, a Jamaican estate manager turned abolitionist, couldn't have been more explicit: 'The cane-holing', he said, 'is a work that calls for very severe exertion and that, I think, must have had a very bad effect upon the female frame. Cane hole digging and night work I considered to be partly the causes of the diminution of the population.'[29]

As manager of a working estate, Taylor would have witnessed the physical effects of this exacting regime first-hand. Accidents aside, it was also responsible for an abnormally high incidence of prolapse, miscarriage, pelvic dislocation, sterility and other gynaecological problems.[30] Consequently, as members of the Barbados Committee lamented in 1789, women slaves were 'very prone' to reproductive disorders that 'often last for their lives'.[31]

Disease, debility, malnutrition and chronic physical exhaustion were a daily fact of life for field hands, and most of the dangers afflicted women and men alike. Insanitary living conditions, sleep deprivation, water polluted by animal and human waste, the effects of corporal punishment and a multitude of life-threatening diseases all took their toll. A study of slave mortality on Jamaica's Worthy Park estate, which looked at the causes of death for just over 400 slaves over a period of forty-six years, identified numerous causes of death. Only one slave in five appears to have died of natural causes.[32]

Pregnant and breastfeeding women were prominent in these death records, as were their children. Several women are listed as having died 'in childbed', and at least one in three of the babies born on the estate was stillborn, 'puny at birth' or dead within the first five years. Others perished during epidemics of measles, smallpox or yellow fever or as a consequence of dysentery, typhoid or malaria. 'Dropsies', suppurating ulcers, yaws, intestinal parasites and pulmonary infections were also common complaints, along with skin diseases, eye infections and other non-fatal conditions. Gonorrhoea was apparently so rife in the slave quarters that it was mostly ignored.

Enslaved people were in dire physical shape, and their diet, high in carbohydrate but low in fats, protein and other essential nutrients, was a major contributing factor. Fed on subsistence rations of rice and horse beans, with a meagre weekly allowance of salt-fish that was often rancid or riddled with worms, most enslaved people suffered from the effects of severe and prolonged malnutrition from an early age. If their daily ration of food amounted to more than 500 calories, they could probably count themselves lucky.[33] This is confirmed in evidence given by planters during an inquiry into the Barbados slave insurrection of 1816. The daily diet of adult field slaves on Barbados's Bayley's and Thickett estates was said to consist of a pint of ginger tea for breakfast, a pound and a half of coo-coo or two pounds of root with peas and vegetables for lunch, plus a pint and a half of guinea corn and five pounds of potatoes or yams. This was supplemented by a weekly allowance of a gill of salt, some pumpkin, a pint and a half of molasses and just one pound of salt fish.[34] There was no mention of any foods containing calcium.

Similar dietary conditions were to be found across the West Indies, but at times of flood, drought or hurricanes, the situation could grow even more desperate. Imported food supplies were not only dependent on the vagaries of the weather, they were also vulnerable to wars, blockades and fluctuating overseas markets. Frequent shortages meant that weekly rations had to be supplemented by any fruits or vegetables that could be cultivated outside working hours. In Jamaica, where land was relatively plentiful, it was fairly common to see people tending their own gardens on Sundays, their one day off. In Barbados, however, where additional land for food crops was in limited supply, field hands experienced frequent periods of semi-starvation. The tiny garden plots attached to their quarters proved inadequate at the best of times. When food was especially scarce, they were left to forage for themselves or steal from neighbouring plantations.

By way of contrast, the diet of most white planters was more likely to result in death from overindulgence. On a visit to Jamaica in 1816, absentee planter Monk Lewis could hardly believe the amount of food he was served at each meal:

> the lord mayor himself need not blush to give his aldermen such a dinner as is placed on my table, even when I dine alone. Land and sea turtle, quails, snipes, plovers, and pigeons and doves of all descriptions . . . excellent pork, barbecued pigs, pepperpots, with numberless other excellent dishes, form the ordinary fare . . . and pineapples make the best tarts that I ever tasted; there is no end of the variety of fruits . . . As to fish,

Savannah la Mar is reckoned the best place in the
island, both for variety and safety . . . and it is only to
be wished that their names equalled their flesh in taste;
for it must be owned, that nothing can be less tempting
than the sounds of Jew-fish, hog-fish, mud-fish, snap-
pers, god-dammies, groupas . . . I never sit down to table
without wishing for the company of Queen Atygatis of
Scythia.[35]

Given the difficulties planters were having in replenishing
the workforce, once the transatlantic trade was abolished, it
was a short-sighted policy to keep their slaves half-starved.
Ironically, Monk Lewis could be heard lamenting the cost
just the day before he described this sumptuous feast. A
woman he'd encountered on his rounds 'had bourne ten
children, and yet has now but one alive: another . . . in the
hospital, has bourne seven and but one has lived to puberty;
and the instances of those who have had four, five, six
children without succeeding in bringing up one, in spite of
the utmost attention and indulgence, are very numerous'.[36]
Among other things, the women he referred to were probably severely malnourished, despite his professed attention
and indulgence.

Although everyone suffered from the effects of an inadequate diet, the consequences for women and girls were
especially drastic, including delayed puberty, irregular or
absent menstruation, premature ageing and a weakened
resistance to infection. The lack of calcium, vitamins and
other nutrients while pregnant or breastfeeding left mothers
more susceptible to rickets, beriberi, oedema and other
life-threatening conditions. For women who somehow

survived pregnancy, these deficiencies helped delay their recovery after childbirth, weakened their breast milk and undermined their capacity to reconceive. Added to this, there was a widespread cultural expectation – one that persists to this day in some Caribbean households – that men should be given the lion's share of any protein.

The impact of such a poor diet on women's fertility and their babies' chances of survival is easily imagined. In an era of widespread medical ignorance, when concepts of hygiene were virtually non-existent, the risks to pregnant and post-natal women would have been phenomenal. Miscarriages and stillbirths aside, the odds of a newborn surviving for more than a few days were abysmal. In Barbados during the 1730s and 1740s, at least half of newborns died before they were one week old. Records from the Codrington estate on Barbados between 1744 and 1748 list twenty-two live births and include at least ten infant deaths. There was Betty's child, who died of 'fitts' when he was ten days old; Molly's boy and Bennebah's girl, both of whom were dead within a week; Joan's daughter, who died at three months; and Occo's daughter, who lasted just five.[37] Of course, the records cannot convey the anguish involved, or the desperate sense of relief that their child had been spared a fate worse than death.

Slave registration records in Grenada suggest that maternal and infant mortality remained high on some islands well into the nineteenth century. In 1817, twenty-eight-year-old Angelique is listed as having died in childbirth and thirty-five-year-old Mary Louise died from 'convulsions after delivery', both on the Morne Fendue estate; Lizette's child died of 'lockjaw' when it was five days old on the Grand Bacolet estate; and on the Hermitage estate, Mary Ermine's child died of measles when it was two months old.[38] The frequency of these fatalities, recorded twenty years after the enactment of legislation that was meant to improve conditions for enslaved women, suggests that old habits had died hard. Giving evidence to the Grenadian Assembly in 1791, John Terry, an overseer of fourteen years, freely admitted that his employers believed 'suckling children should die for they lost a great deal of the mother's work during the infancy of the child'.[39] Such attitudes were all too common, despite planters' protests to the contrary.

Eventually, the tendency to value women's capacity to work over their capacity to breed would have serious consequences for their owners. Among other things, it generated an alarming decline in the birth rate – a situation that proved largely irreversible despite the introduction of dietary improvements toward the end of the eighteenth century. Breeding incentives, lying-in hospitals and other efforts to improve conditions for pregnant and nursing mothers proved too little, too late. In contrast to the American South, which had experienced a steady natural increase over the years,[40] the slave population on West Indian sugar colonies continued to plummet.

As abolitionist arguments gained ground, the declining slave population caused mounting concern. On nearly every island, efforts were made to reverse this negative trend. Yet to the puzzlement and exasperation of the planters, the number of slaves who perished continued to outweigh the number born. Having seen how appallingly they were treated, it seems logical to blame the women's diet and material conditions and to look no further. But to do so would be to ignore the tantalising evidence that some enslaved women, by seizing the little control they could exercise over their own bodies, found conscious, subversive ways to sabotage their owners' shameful project.

A treadmill scene in Jamaica, wood engraving, 1834 (Granger Historical Picture Archive)

4

Equal under the Whip: Punishment and Coercion

[B]ookkeepers and overseers kick black women in the belly from one end of Jamaica to the other.

Matthew 'Monk' Lewis,
Journal of a West India Proprietor (London, 1834)

Slavery in the British West Indies lasted well over 200 years. It hardly needs stating that such prolonged physical abuse could not have been sustained without the use of corporal and capital punishment and a range of other coercive measures. Outnumbered and ever fearful of rebellion, planters did everything in their power to ensure that the slightest hint of defiance was quashed before it could spread. Despite this, there is a weight of evidence that fear alone could not quash the desire for freedom. Wherever rumours of emancipation circulated, revolt and insurrection followed, ushering in yet more repression.

In a letter from General Murray, tasked with investigating the causes of the Demerara rebellion of 1823, this refusal of the enslaved to accept their state of bondage was eloquently described:

> I expostulated the beneficent views of His Majesty for bettering their condition; explained the abolition of the flogging of female slaves and the carrying of whips in the field as but the first steps to the intended measures. These things, they said, were no comfort to them; God had made them of the same flesh and blood as the whites; they were tired of being slaves; their good King had sent orders that they should be free, and they would not work any more.

Clearly, the promise that things would improve over time was unacceptable.[1]

Enslaved people would have been under no illusion about the risks involved. The odds were stacked against them, and the consequences were dire. The Jamaican Assembly blatantly endorsed execution and torture, including slow starvation, burning to death, amputation of hands, feet, tongues or ears, the rubbing of salt, pepper or hot wax into lacerated skin, and the prolonged use of iron chain weights, thumbscrews and other physical restraints. Punishment in the eighteenth and nineteenth centuries was typically sadistic and many of these methods were by no means exclusive to slaves. Back in England, they were still publicly disembowelling people and sticking felons' heads on spikes. Nevertheless, West Indian laws were notoriously biased in the interests of planters, and the use of excessive violence was condoned almost as a matter of principle.

The violence meted out to the enslaved was casual, indiscriminate and way over the top. Planters and overseers made regular use of the whip on people they suspected of shirking, malingering or lagging behind, including field labourers who collapsed from exhaustion. Individuals could be placed in the stocks or in solitary confinement for days or weeks at a time, often for the pettiest of crimes. Repeat offenders would be forced to work in chains or wear neck irons that prevented them from lying down, while amputation was used as a common disincentive for runaways. These measures had the full backing of the law which, until Whitehall stepped in, was both determined and administered by local whites-only assemblies.

For much of the period of slavery, these assemblies were a law unto themselves. In Bermuda, for example, legislation passed in 1730 made Europeans exempt from execution or fines for killing a slave, yet if a slave so much as threatened a white man, the offence was punishable by death. The murder of a slave did not become a capital offence in the West Indies until 1804. It would be another twenty-two years before the Consolidated Slave Law, an attempt to standardise legislation across the British Caribbean, acknowledged that a black woman could be raped. Until then, the very worst a white rapist could expect was a modest fine – in other words, a slap on the wrist.

It goes without saying that the use of physical coercion had to be reinforced by the psychology of fear. The threat of permanent separation from family and children was ever-present, for it usually meant sale or transportation to another colony. This served both as a penalty for persistent or incendiary misbehaviour and as an eloquent warning to others. In Barbados in 1721, an absentee landlord who had received reports of laziness and malingering ordered his manager to transport any slaves whom he considered 'a . . . discouragement to the industriousness of others'. After a lengthy search for a buyer, four 'lazy women' were sold to a merchant from Virginia on the American mainland and transported several thousand miles away from their friends and family, including any children they may have had.[2] One convicted woman was even sent to Australia – a 25-year-old domestic who was accused of slipping arsenic into the food of her master and his family. Perhaps because she didn't succeed in killing them, she was spared execution and transported instead to the penal colony of New South Wales.[3] Whether she lived to tell her tale to the equally brutalised Aborigines we'll never know, but it's an intriguing scenario.

Mary Prince never forgot the trauma of being 'sold away'. Born in Bermuda in 1788, she was just twelve years old when she and her two younger sisters were wrenched from their mother and sold to different owners. Her account of the experience, dismissed by some at the time as abolitionist propaganda, gives moving insight into what it was like to be on the receiving end of such callous treatment:

The black morning came; it came too soon for my poor mother and us. Whilst she was putting on us the new osnaburgs in which we were to be sold, she said, in a sorrowful voice, (I shall never forget it!) 'See, I am shrouding my poor children; what a task for a mother! I am going to carry my little chickens to market,' (these were her exact words) 'take your last look of them' . . . With my sisters we reached Hamble Town about four o'clock in the afternoon; we followed mother to the market-place, where she placed us in a row against a large house, with our backs to the wall and our arms folded in front. I stood first, Hannah next to me, then Dinah; and our mother stood beside us crying. My heart throbbed with grief and terror so violently that I pressed my hands tightly across my breast, but couldn't keep it still, and it continued to leap as though it would burst out of my body. But who cared for that? Did any of the bystanders think of the pain that wrung the hearts of the Negro woman and her young ones? No, no! They weren't all bad, I dare say, but slavery hardens white people's hearts towards the blacks. At length the auctioneer arrived and asked my mother which was the eldest. She pointed to me. He took me by the hand, and led me out into the middle of the street. I was soon surrounded by strange men, who examined and handled me like a butcher with a calf or a lamb he was about to purchase, and who talked about my shape and size as if I couldn't understand what they were saying. I was then put up to sale. The bidding commenced at a few pounds, and gradually rose to fifty-seven. People said that I'd fetched a great sum for so young a slave. I then saw my sisters sold to different owners. When the sale was over, my mother hugged and kissed us, and mourned over us, begging us to keep a good heart, and to do our duty to our new masters. It was a sad parting; one went one way, one another, and our poor mammy went home with nothing.[4]

There is no mention in Mary's account of being branded with a hot iron, although this method of denoting a change of ownership was common practice.

Enslaved people lived under a constant reign of terror, and surviving punishment records confirm that no concessions were made to women. Although white women were seen at the time as the 'weaker' sex, their black sisters were effectively discounted, in keeping with the view that Africans and their descendants were not fully human. Answerable to their absent employers, attorneys and estate managers were often required to keep detailed records of the chastisements they meted out. Women are prominent in the lists of slaves whom owners and managers wanted taught a lesson, typically with the sanction or collusion of local magistrates. Among the alleged offences, there are numerous references to insolence, disobedience, laziness, quarrelling, shirking, theft and disorderly conduct. Their lists confirm that women were regularly, repeatedly and disproportionately punished, and that they were also persistent offenders, despite the fearful repercussions.

Flogging, most often administered by a fellow slave in the presence of the owner or his agent, required the victim to be stripped and physically restrained. Usually they would be made to lie prone on the ground to receive the required number of lashes, but there were some sadistic variations. While on a military expedition in Surinam, soldier John Stedman tried to intervene when he witnessed an eighteen-year-old girl being literally flayed alive, 'tied up by both arms to a tree, as naked as she came into the world . . . from her neck to her ancles [sic] literally dyed over in blood'. The girl had already received 200 lashes, but her punishment was doubled for 'firmly refusing to submit to the loathsome embraces of her detestable executioner'.[5]

Whipping was not confined to adults.[6] Mary Prince describes how she learnt from an early age 'the exact difference between the smart of the rope, the cart-whip and the cow-skin, when applied to my naked body'. She was also regularly assaulted by her mistress with 'dreadful . . . blows received on my face and head from her hard, heavy fist'.[7] Such arbitrary abuse probably went unrecorded, but there are numerous eyewitness accounts that corroborate her description of the harsh way slaves were treated, regardless of age or gender.

Pregnant women could be subjected to these punishments too, although to avoid unnecessary losses, if sentenced to death it was common practice to delay the execution until after the birth of her child. When flogged, a hole would be dug to accommodate the woman's swollen belly. Abolitionist Thomas Cooper, travelling in Jamaica in the 1820s, was outraged when he witnessed the punishment of two women, both of them pregnant, who had asked to be allowed to leave the field during a bout of heavy rain. When the overseer refused, 'they went to complain . . . to a magistrate, but were stopped in their way by a neighbouring overseer and . . . thrown into the stocks until he sent them back to their own overseer, who put them again into the stocks on their own estate, and had them flogged'.[8] Clearly, women could not rely on the protection of the law, even when pregnant. If anything, these two women probably received a heavier punishment for having the cheek to complain.

Following parliamentary legislation in 1826 that sought to ban the flogging of women, a spell in the 'hand and foot' stocks or a period of solitary confinement provided alternative ways of punishing recalcitrant women, as did the treadmill. But since women could still be lawfully flogged on the private order of their owners, use of the whip remained widespread and probably went under-reported. Punishment records from the Baillies Bacolet plantation in Grenada include a reference to Eliza, a field worker, who was given twenty lashes in 1823 for 'violent conduct and excessive insolence'. Ten years later on the same estate, Germaine was given fifteen lashes for 'wilfully destroying canes in the field and general neglect of duty'.[9] Examples such as these are found in records on every island. They confirm that on many estates, the whip continued to be used with impunity even after the enslaved had technically been freed.

Penalties for the most serious crimes (such as murder, insurrection or running away) usually involved an element of torture, sometimes resulting in a slow, excruciating death. In 1828, a group of enslaved women who were found guilty of discontent and mutiny in St Lucia, were 'hung by the arms to a peg, raised so high above their heads, that the toes alone touched the ground, the whole weight of the body resting on the wrists of the arms and tips of the toes'.[10] Runaways risked mutilation, including facial disfigurement and the amputation of toes, feet or other body parts, to discourage further attempts. While this did not necessarily kill them, the resulting haemorrhage or infection often did.

Death may not always have been the intention when a punishment was inflicted, but it was frequently the outcome. In 1799, when visiting Farmer's plantation in Barbados, a Mr Joseph Senhouse witnessed two women millworkers who had been chained together for an unspecified offence. 'One of them', he records, 'unfortunately reaching too near the Rollers, her fingers were caught between them and her body was drawn through the mill. The iron chain, being seized by the rollers, was likewise drawn through and . . . the other female negroe was dragg'd so close to those cylinders that her head was severed from her body.'[11]

There are few accounts by those on the receiving end of these vile coercive practices. In a rare account of conditions in Jamaica's workhouses shortly after Emancipation in 1834, James Williams, an eighteen-year-old ex-slave-turned-apprentice, gave a sickening description of the conditions that, if anything, had worsened since slavery was abolished. His account describes how, having been found guilty by the magistrate of some trite offence, he was made to 'dance the treadmill' with other newly 'freed slaves'. Introduced throughout the British West Indies as a 'normal corrective expedient', the treadmill was meant to be an alternative to whipping. His description of its severe and callous use serves as yet another graphic reminder, if ever such were needed, that neither age, gender nor pregnancy incited an iota of compassion:

There was one old woman with grey head, belong to Mr Wallace and she could not dance the mill at all: she hang by the two wrists which was strapped to the bar, and the driver kept on flogging her. She get more than

all the rest, her clothes cut off with the Cat, the shoulder
strap cut with it and her shift hang down over that side;
then they flog upon that shoulder and cut it up very bad.
But all the flogging couldn't make she dance the mill
and when she come down all her back covered with
blood. They keep on putting her on the mill for a week
and flog her every time . . . There was a great many
woman in the workhouse, and several have sucking child;
and there was one woman quite big with child, and them
make her dance the mill too, morning and evening. She
not able to dance good and them flog her; she complain
about her stomach hurt her, and I see her several time go
and beg the overseer not to work her on the mill, but
him say not him send her there . . . All the woman that
not able to dance was flog most dreadful . . . There was
twenty-one woman from Hiattsfield . . . several of them
have young children. I think they was in for fourteen
days . . . I hear the list call and counted the people . . .
(by) the Tuesday, there was only three of these women
able to work in the field, all the rest was in the hospital
from being cut up with the mill and the flogging; them
all look quite shocking when them let out, some hardly
able to walk to go home. The most lively among them
was all mashed up with the mill, all the skin bruised off
her shin. She had a young child too: she tell me she was
put in the workhouse three weeks before and now them
send her back again.[12]

Across Europe, the insatiable demand for sugar to sweeten
the coffee of those who could afford to drink it made resort
to the treadmill, the stocks, confinement and other forms of

punishment inevitable. How else were West Indian planters to maintain a compliant workforce? Black women's bodies suffered cruelly as they bore the brunt of these harsh disciplinary policies. As late as 1832, William Taylor, a plantation doctor, testified to the House of Common's Select Committee that corporal punishment was a frequent cause of miscarriage among women field slaves.[13]

Field hands were not the only victims. The diet and working conditions of domestic slaves may have been marginally less debilitating, but they were rarely out of sight and so under constant scrutiny. Maids and housekeepers risked arbitrary punishment for the most trivial offences. They also lived in constant fear of being sent to work in the fields. An example of their vulnerability was provided by Reverend Henry Coor who, as a house guest in Jamaica in the 1780s, witnessed the nailing of a house-wench's ear to a tree for breaking a plate.[14] In Barbados, a domestic nearly lost an ear when her irate master attempted to chop it off with a machete for gossiping about something he suspected she'd overheard.[15] In San Domingo, where the slave-force was in theory protected by the French *Code Noir*, a careless cook was reportedly thrown into the oven by her irate mistress – a woman otherwise described as 'beautiful, rich and very much admired'.[16]

For those who worked in the house, experiences like this seem to have been commonplace. Mary Prince, transported by her owners from one island to another, gave a chilling account of the perils of life as a domestic servant:

My mistress sent me round the corner of the house to empty a large earthen jar. The jar was already cracked with an old deep crack that divided it in the middle, and in turning it upside down to empty it, it parted in my hand. I could not help the accident, but I was dreadfully frightened, looking forward to a severe punishment. I ran crying to my mistress, 'O mistress, the jar has come in two'. 'You have broken it, have you?' she replied; 'come directly here to me'. I came trembling: she stripped and flogged me long and severely with the cowskin; as long as she had strength to use the lash, for she did not give over till she was quite tired. When my master came home at night, she told him of my fault; and oh, frightful! How he fell to swearing. After abusing me with every ill name he could think of . . . and giving me several heavy blows with his hand, he said 'I shall come home tomorrow at twelve, on purpose to give you a round hundred'. He kept his word – Oh sad for me! I cannot easily forget it. He tied me upon a ladder, and gave me a hundred lashes with his own hand, and master Benjy stood by to count them for him. When he had licked me for some time he sat down to take breath; then after resting, he beat me again and again, until he was quite wearied, and so hot (for the weather was very sultry) that he sank back in his chair, like to faint . . . I crawled away on my hands and knees and laid myself down under the steps of the piazza in front of the house. I was in a dreadful state – my body all blood and bruises . . . The next morning, I was forced by my master to rise and go about my usual work, though my body and limbs were so stiff and sore that I could not move without the greatest pain. Nevertheless, even after all this severe punishment, I never heard the last of that jar, my mistress was always throwing it in my face.[17]

The effect on Mary's health proved so severe that by her late teens, her body was bent and broken. While in Bermuda, her master, 'taking off his heavy boot . . . struck me such a severe blow in the small of my back, that I shrieked with agony and thought I was killed'. The assault left her with back problems that plagued her for the rest of her life.[18]

Mary Prince's complex relationship with her owners hints at a perverse and sadistic psychology. Her mistress thought nothing of stripping her naked 'to hang me up by the wrists and lay my flesh open with the cow-skin', which she describes as 'an ordinary punishment for even a slight offence'. Nor was she averse to keeping Mary up all night to wash clothes or 'pick wool and cotton', resulting in severe sleep deprivation. Mary describes several other occasions when both her master and mistress beat her to the point of physical exhaustion.

If her account is to be believed (and only those sceptics who opposed abolition suggested it wasn't), the argument that domestic slaves had an easier time under slavery is deeply flawed. For maids, cooks and housekeepers, any comforts or privileges attached to their marginally superior status were all but cancelled out by their precarious position. As easy prey to the sadistic whims of those they served, it should come as no surprise that throughout the period of slavery, almost as many domestics are known to have run away as field slaves.[19]

White mistresses such as Mary's were a common sight in Barbados, although relatively scarce on other islands. And they were notoriously spiteful. Control of domestic servants was probably one of the few arenas in which they could exercise any real power, and they seem to have made the most of it. Their isolated lives – often on remote plantations surrounded by slaves they dared not trust and controlled by abusive husbands or fathers – would have left them in a constant state of paranoia. Their feelings of insecurity were no doubt aggravated by the sexual excesses of their menfolk, both residents and house guests, toward the black or brown females in the household. This spawned a particular kind of vindictiveness, especially when a mistress harboured feelings of jealousy or resentment toward an attractive female slave. Soldier John Stedman witnessed such behaviour first-hand: 'I have seen the most cruel tortures inflicted for submitting to the desire of a husband . . . from the false accusations of a lustful (white) woman, prompted alone by jealousy'.[20]

The correspondence of Elizabeth Fenwick, an English-woman who established a school for white children in Bridgetown, Barbados, at the start of the nineteenth century, gives a telling glimpse into her relationship with enslaved female domestics. In letters to a woman friend in England written between 1814 and 1821, she complains that 'no imagination can form an idea of the unceasing turmoil and vexation their management causes . . . I was several times almost mad with the provocations their dirt, disobedience and dishonesty caused me'. Fenwick found slavery 'horrid' and claims to have abstained from using the whip, but there is no love lost between her and her domes-tics. Her efforts to control them had little effect. 'To kindness and forbearance they return insolence and contempt', she insists. 'Nothing awes or governs them but the lash of the whip or the dread of being sent into the fields to labour.'[21]

Her letters also reveal just how oppressive the lives of some white women in the colonies could be. For years, her daughter Eliza was unhappily married to a Mr R., who, like so many of his peers, drank to excess. Eventually, when his mother-in-law confronted him, he set sail for England, abandoning Eliza 'exactly one hour after she was put to Bed of her fourth Child'. Fenwick speaks of the relief her daughter felt at 'no longer being exhausted with nights of watching, shame and terror of what evils intoxication might involve her in before dawn'; Eliza's joy on seeing her children 'saved from witness-ing the errors of their father' and her liberation from any more unwanted pregnancies seems to outweigh any concerns she might have had about her new status as an abandoned woman with four children to raise.[22] It is hard to discern whether her experience was typical, but it sheds an interesting light on the psychology of some white women, who, hardened by their own miserable experiences, apparently thought nothing of taking out their frustrations on their slaves.

Following their example, free 'coloured' women were also known for their excessive cruelty toward female domestics. Desperate to distance themselves from the taint of slavery and raised to feel ashamed of their African roots, their attempts to emulate white society included dress, manner-isms and behaviour. Relationships between free 'coloureds' and the enslaved were complex, particularly in a society so obsessed with skin colour and social status. The presence of a maid who could well have been a mother or grandmother would have been an unwelcome reminder to these women of their own lowly origins.

In Barbados, where black, brown and white women formed over half the population for nigh on two centuries, the risk of such encounters was especially high. Registration data from 1817 lists over 56 per cent of the 'coloured' female population and nearly 70 per cent of the black female population as domestics. But neither freedom nor inherited wealth gave them access to the privileges enjoyed by affluent white women, who regarded 'yellow' skin as an unwelcome reminder of their husbands' and fathers' adultery. For all their assumed airs and graces, they were trapped within a rigid pigmentocracy in which it was 'a universal principal of Colonial law that any person of colour is assumed to be a Slave and the onus is on the person of colour to prove he or she is free'.[23] Shunned by respectable white society and both despised and envied by the enslaved, many of these free women of colour found themselves caught between a rock and a hard place. Again, it was their domestics who bore the brunt of their frustration.

Women were clearly a convenient punching bag, yet accounts of the treatment of black and so-called 'coloured' men are no less horrifying. In a context where violent and sadistic punishment was the rule rather than the exception, they could be killed or castrated for merely looking at a white woman. In their encounters with planters and overseers, men suffered daily acts of brutality regardless of status, and the threat posed by their masculinity meant that the punishments they received for minor misdemeanours were often all out of proportion to the crime. Biology alone spared them the additional physical toll of menstruation, pregnancy, childbirth, breastfeeding, menopause and the ever-present threat of rape. There were undoubtedly exceptions, particularly where prospective 'studs' or attractive young boys were concerned, but it is fair to assume that a majority of men on the plantation escaped the trauma of casual and repeated sexual abuse from all comers.

Women and girls, on the other hand, were prey to the sexual whims of both their fellow slaves and white estate managers – men who used sexual coercion not just to satisfy their sexual urges but to repress the free will of the enslaved. An effective form of control, it was a way of demonstrating their absolute power to use and abuse their 'property' as they saw fit. Not all women succumbed without a fight. Reverend John Barry's evidence to the House of Lords Select Committee in 1832 referred to women who were 'subjected to corporal punishment for non-compliance with the libidinous desires of the person in authority on the estate'. He went on to denounce the widespread practice of overseers and bookkeepers who, on Sunday visits, were in the habit of '(having) women selected upon the properties for the purpose of sleeping with . . . visitors'.[24]

It was not just white men who were guilty of such excesses. James Williams described how 'the drivers constant try to get after the young women . . . even them that married, no matter'. One young woman, Amelia Lawrence, 'complain to her brother and me, that never one morning pass without the driver after her – she don't know what to do, she quite hurt and disheartened about it'. Yet despite the absolute power this man must have wielded over her, 'she did not give way'.[25] Williams' account suggests that some perpetrators took a perverse sexual pleasure in targeting defenceless women. 'One day . . . two young woman was sent in from Moneague side . . . them don't know how to dance the mill, them flog them so severe, they cut away most of their clothes, and left them in a manner naked; and the driver was bragging afterwards that he see all their nakedness'.[26]

Unlike enslaved women, who could not complain to anyone, white women complained bitterly about the decadent behaviour of their menfolk. On her visit to St Kitts and Antigua in 1774, Scotswoman Janet Shaw was shocked to see 'crouds of Mullatoes, which you meet in the streets and houses . . . indeed everywhere'. As a tourist with little insight into the sexual politics of the plantation, she was quick to blame the 'young black wenches' for the men's behaviour. '(They) lay themselves out for their white lovers', she fumed, '(and) become licentious and insolent beyond all bearing'.[27]

Elizabeth Fenwick, who was resident in Barbados for seven years, saw things slightly differently. She blamed 'the vices of Manhood' and 'a horrid and disgraceful System' that encouraged female slaves into prostitution. Mindful of the dangers to her son in such a morally lax environment, she wrote:

The Gentlemen are greatly addicted to their women slaves & give the fruit of their licentiousness to their white children as slaves. I strongly suspect that a very fine Mulatto boy about 14 who comes here to help wait on two young Ladies, our pupils, is their own brother, from the likeness he bears to their father. It is a common case & not thought of as an enormity. It gives me a disgusted antipathy & I am ready to hail the Slave and reject the Master.[28]

Back in Britain, reports of plantation debauchery were both a source of titillation and a subject of growing debate. As public outrage gathered momentum, it became a favourite subject of coffee house gossip, broadsheets and anti-slavery tracts. In an article entitled *The 'Ruin' of Jamaica*, a certain Mr R. Hildreth berated the plantocracy for their hedonistic lifestyle, which he described as consisting of 'wine, brandy, ale, rum and black mistresses'.[29] His opinion of his fellow white men was far from complimentary. 'Their only relaxations' he railed, 'were drunken frolics, naked Negro girls being employed to wait at table; while it was an ordinary piece of Jamaica hospitality to furnish, not only a bed to the guest, but a woman to share it'.

Predictably, Hildreth blames these sexual excesses on the men's proximity to Africans. Still, his insights into the predicament of concubines and mistresses are uncharacteristically sympathetic:

The females had as their only resource the concubinage above described – a degraded position in which, however, they often fulfilled, with the utmost scrupulousness and self-devotion, all the duties, without enjoying one of the rights of a wife . . . the enjoyments, if they are to be called such, secured by it to the limited white population, and to them only, being of the grossest character. From living constantly among Negroes, mostly imported from Africa, over whom they exercised despotic authority, the white immigrants, the greater part of them not over-refined to begin with, degenerated into gross barbarians.[30]

The easy access that white men assumed over black and brown women's bodies was so 'normal' in the context of slavery, there's been a tendency to overlook the trauma of being exposed to such sexual excess on a daily basis. Some historians prefer the idea that enslaved women took readily to rape and prostitution while black men looked sullenly on. They present an image of slave society in which female promiscuity and licentiousness were the norm – an environment in which slave mothers wielded great influence as pimps, while 'hot constitution'd' young women, unable to resist the promise of favouritism or prestige, offered their favours freely to all comers in exchange for trinkets.[31]

Promiscuity, prostitution and sexual manipulation were, without doubt, one aspect of the sexual dynamics on the plantation. After all, this was one of the few arenas in which established power relations between slave owner and slave could be stood on their head. But it is evidence supplied by contemporary white men that has given this stereotype such lasting credibility. It was hardly in the interests of planters to concede that perversion or debauchery, much less genuine affection, might have characterised their relationships with such women. Instead they accused them of moral degeneracy and lewd, lascivious behaviour, inspired by 'dark passions' that lured the hapless white man into a state of lost innocence.

Commenting on these practices in Jamaica in the late eighteenth century, the views of Edward Long were typical. European men, he argued, were 'used to greater purity and strictness of manners' and thus 'too easily led aside to give loose to every kind of sensual delight'. He blamed their moral downfall on the wiles of 'some black or yellow quasheeba, by whom a tawny breed is produced'.[32] However, Mary Prince, speaking for countless silenced women, tells a very different story.[33] Describing her master's 'ugly fashion of stripping himself quite naked and ordering me then to wash him in a tub of water', she insists that 'this was worse to me than all the licks'.

A rare insight into the nature and scale of this sexual abuse is provided in the intimate journals of Thomas Thistlewood, who was employed as an overseer in Jamaica between 1750 and 1786.[34] In the space of two years, while employed on the Vineyard estate, he records having sexual intercourse with no less than eleven of the eighteen women slaves. As well as his resident favourite Marina, who was rewarded with money and clothing, Thistlewood claims that he frequently lay with other women in the open fields and slave huts when the mood took him. His stated preference was for young, newly arrived African girls, who were evidently confronted with his sexual demands as part of the seasoning process.[35]

Thistlewood continued to chronicle his exploits at the Egypt plantation, where he secured his second contract. He records having sex with at least a dozen women, despite being afflicted with a particularly nasty combination of gonorrhoea and buboes, a condition that required him to take four months' leave at the end of 1752. For the majority of Thistlewood's conquests, the only long-term benefits, it seems, were the risks of unwelcome pregnancy and venereal disease. The notion that women would have welcomed such 'rewards' belongs to the realms of pornographic fantasy. Far from being rendered more amenable, his victims would have found it hard to distinguish his unwanted attentions from the many other forms of coercion devised by agents and magistrates to enforce their submission.

Enslaved men may not have fallen victim to these particular horrors themselves, but they undoubtedly witnessed them. Like vanquished males throughout history, they would have experienced the sexual conquest of their mothers, sisters, daughters and loved ones as a calculated affront to their manhood, and with good reason. Thistlewood boasted of having intercourse with seven out of eight newly arrived African women, three of whom were listed in plantation records as living in the households of males. At least two of his conquests were described as living with male slaves, possibly as husband and wife. It seems unlikely that these men would have simply shrugged their shoulders. A more likely scenario is that their rage in the face of such symbolic emasculation would have generated feelings of blame, fury and impotence, with untold repercussions for themselves and their hapless partners.

So, the myth that women had an easier time under slavery because they spent it on their backs can be firmly laid to rest. Whether in the fields or in the great house, enslaved women were vulnerable to every possible form of abuse and exploitation. The evidence conjures an image of a life that was both physically and mentally ruinous for all but a privileged few. That anyone survived such prolonged brutalisation is nothing short of a miracle. Their condition is best conveyed by planter Monk Lewis, who observed in his diary during a visit in 1817 that

I have not passed six months in Jamaica, and I have already found on one of my estates a woman who had

been kicked in the womb by a white book-keeper, by
which she was crippled herself, and on another of my
estates another woman who had been kicked in the
womb by another white book-keeper, by which he had
crippled the child . . . and thus, as my two estates are at
the two extremities of the island, I am entitled to say,
from my own knowledge . . . that white book-keepers
kick black women in the belly from one end of Jamaica
to the other.[36]

Of course, the possibility that gender may have rendered
women's suffering more acute has important implications.
For if a person's motivation to resist bears any relationship
to the weight of their oppression, it could be argued that,
collectively, enslaved women had an even greater incentive
than men to undermine the system. Whatever their motives,
recalcitrant women became a force with which to be
reckoned. Their options may have been limited, but there is
evidence to suggest that they used every last means at their
disposal to fight back.

Woman in the stocks, wood engraving, 1846

5

Enslaved Women and Subversion: The Violence of Turbulent Women

The females compose the most numerous and effective part of the field gangs of the estate; from the indulgences already extended to them they have shown themselves to be the most turbulent description of the slaves, and would become perfectly unmanageable if they knew that this description of correction was abolished by law. It is therefore absolutely necessary (for the present) that it should be held in terror over them. If suddenly prohibited it is impossible to say what might be the consequences.[1]

President Paterson of Grenada,
writing to Earl Bathurst, 23 November 1825

Enslaved women were by no means the passive victims we've been led to believe, despite the extremity of their lives. They contributed their full share to the long tradition of resistance that was such a striking feature of slavery throughout the British West Indies. Punishment lists and court records confirm that they presented a major discipline problem to their captors, who complained loudly and long about the insolence and incorrigibility of women they were at a loss to control. The ever-present threat of repression was no match for the dreams and resentments of 'turbulent' women, whose responses ranged from small daily acts of non-cooperation to major acts of rebellion.

Planter Monk Lewis, whose 'indulgences' toward his slaves were openly frowned upon by his fellow planters, made several references in his diary to the uncooperative behaviour of his women slaves. One of his housemaids stubbornly refused to open the blinds, despite repeated requests. 'The girl . . . whose business it is to open the house each morning', he complained, 'has in vain been desired to unclose all the jalousies: she never fails to leave three or four closed, and when she is scolded for doing so, she takes care to open those three the next morning and leaves shut the opposite side'.[2] We can almost see the furtive smile playing on this anonymous girl's lips as she feigned stupidity – a small act of defiance, maybe, but enough to infuriate her owner. Another woman, a field hand by the name of Jenny who was recovering from an accident, insisted on returning to the hospital after absconding to tend to her provision grounds. When refused readmittance, she went to the extremes of reinfecting her hand, tying packthread around it and rubbing dirt into the wound in order to receive her full entitlement of convalescence.[3]

Monk Lewis also had cause to complain about a 'Petticoat Rebellion', when the women labourers on his estate downed tools and 'one and all refused to carry away the trash . . . without the slightest pretence'. The mill was shut down for

Ana Nzinga, Angolan Queen

Dahomey Amazons, 1891

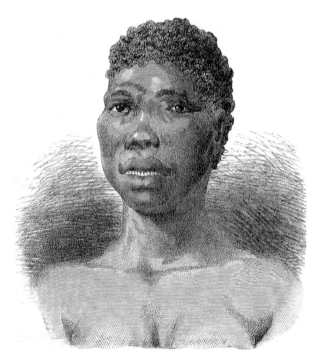

Saartje Baartman, the Hottentot Venus, South Africa, 1890 (Antiqua Print Gallery)

The torture of a female slave, 1792 Abolitionist Leaflet

Image of Joanna, 1838 – from the
Frontispiece of Stedman's Narrative

Nanny of the Maroons, as she appears
on the Jamaican 500 dollar note

several days, yet the women stubbornly refused to go back to work. When the driver attempted to persuade them, 'a fierce young devil of a Miss Whaunica flew at his throat and endeavoured to strangle him'. Lewis, who regarded himself as quite a placid man, admits that he lost his temper and 'bounced and stormed for half an hour with all (his) might and main'. Yet his fury made little impression on these feisty, intractable women. Again, we can almost see them standing there, arms crossed, refusing to budge. His agent insisted that they all deserved a good flogging: 'Every morning (he) regales me with some fresh instance of insubordination . . . and evidently gives me to understand that the estate cannot be properly governed without the cartwhip . . . I have in consequence assured the women that since they will not be managed by fair treatment, I must have recourse to other measures'.[4]

The threat of physical punishment was clearly no more effective than the act in quelling their defiance. With nothing to lose, even the threat of death lost its power. During a visit to a slave court in 1816, Lewis was struck by the flippancy of Minelta, a fifteen-year-old girl on trial for attempting to poison her master. 'On being condemned to death', he wrote, 'she heard the sentence without the least emotion; and . . . when she went down the steps of the court house, she was seen to laugh.'[5]

Such blatant irreverence sent a shiver down the spine of planters and overseers, for it proved that, however hard they tried, they were incapable of suppressing the free will of those they'd enslaved. Complaints of widespread malingering, insubordination, strikes and physical assaults by women suggest that a significant number were prepared to risk

everything, including life itself, to assert their claim to some
form of personal agency. As late as 1826, Jamaican laws
limiting the number of lashes that could be inflicted on
slaves made no concessions to women. Indeed, as public
pressure to abolish the whip gathered momentum back
home, planters and governors throughout the British West
Indies could be heard warning of the dire consequences,
especially for their control of non-compliant women.

Sir Ralph Woodward, who was governor of Trinidad in
the 1820s, made one such impassioned plea for the whip to
be retained. It was the women, he insisted, who were most
prone to give offence. In 1823, members of the Barbados
Council echoed his sentiments, claiming that 'Black ladies
have rather a tendency to the Amazonian cast of character'.
In Grenada, planters protested that women would become
'perfectly unmanageable' if they could no longer be flogged.
And when, despite their protests, the use of the whip was
finally abolished, Woodward wrote to the colonial secretary
in London, lamenting that he no longer possessed the
authority to 'repress the violence of turbulent women'.

Enslaved women had certainly earned their reputation for
being unmanageable. The anonymous woman field hand
who was said by Monk Lewis to have 'flown at the overseer
with the greatest fury (and) grasped him by the neck',
prevailing on her fellow slaves to ' "Dunbar" him',[6] (a reference to the fate of Mr Dunbar, an overseer who was
murdered by slaves on a neighbouring plantation) seems a
far cry from the Hollywood-inspired image of the docile
female slave, prevented from retaliation by her servile nature
and the constraints of her gender. In reality, women's sexual

disadvantage could be the key to understanding their defiance. They may have been 'equal under the whip', but planters' efforts to dehumanise them were fiercely and creatively resisted.

Clearly not all women were brave or heroic. Some resigned themselves to their fate and resolved to make the best of it; others will have chosen to collude and would have taken full advantage of any perks, often in the interests of children or family members. Concubines and mistresses are often so accused, yet like their predecessors in Africa's forts and barracoons, their sexual availability did not necessarily bring them the special concessions they'd hoped. With so few white women available for marriage, the taking of a black or brown mistress was common practice among planters and agents. But as John Stedman observed in his memoirs, such relationships were not necessarily based on the woman's consent:

> If a Negro and his wife have ever so great an attachment for each other, the woman, if handsome, must yield to the loathsome embrace of an adulterous and licentious manager, or see her husband cut to pieces for endeavouring to prevent it. This in frequent instances has driven them to distraction and been the cause of many murders.[7]

Stedman's sympathy with the 'husband' may stem from first-hand experience. Based in the Dutch colony of Surinam between 1772 and 1777, where he had been sent to fight the Maroons, he formed a deep attachment with a 'mulatto' woman named Joanna. After his beloved mistress was indecently assaulted by another soldier in his platoon, she repulsed him, and left 'the marks of her just resentment on his face'. Stedman's devotion to Joanna appears genuine, and he is a rare example of a white man who was not afraid to admit it. Yet she was evidently a woman who knew her own mind. Although Stedman married her and eventually succeeded in purchasing freedom for his wife and young son, he was unable to persuade her to return with him to Holland.

Enslaved women were mostly lured into relationships with white men by the promise of more favourable treatment or eventually being given their freedom, even though they risked being socially ostracised. According to Edward Long, who dismissed them as 'so many leeches', some of these women used their seductive powers to the full, 'persuading the man she detests to believe she is most violently smitten with the beauty of his person'.[8] From the vantage point of men who took their fill of this 'forbidden fruit', such cynicism is understandable. The idea that black and brown women could manipulate them by turning established power relations on their head would have been disconcerting, to say the least. In contrast, Elizabeth Fenwick, as a schoolmistress in Barbados for seven years from 1814, viewed these relationships with a woman's sensibility. To her, they were victims of 'a horrid and disgraceful system' that encouraged female slaves into prostitution.

The popular stereotype of the favoured 'mulatto' mistress who identified with her white lover at the expense of her fellow slaves reveals only one possible facet of her experience. As one historian put it,

> for every pampered planter's favourite whose children were freed and educated abroad, for every ten faithful

Phibbas, there were a hundred more like Mulatto Kitty
at Worthy Park, with her eight children by five different
fathers (three white and two black); none of her offspring
were manumitted . . . [And] many others like Mary
Anne, the mulatto daughter of Sukey Lowe, who went to
work for the bookkeepers almost as a matter of course,
bore a quadroon child at the age of seventeen and was
turned back into the field once she became permanently
sick with a menstrual disorder. Thereafter, with her two
half-brothers she formed a trio of notably 'ill-disposed'
and troublesome slaves.[9]

Mary Anne's ill-disposed-ness provides rare insight into the
mindset of enslaved women. In her case, the experience of
sexual exploitation from an early age seems to have had the
effect of *hardening* rather than reducing her opposition to
slavery. Her plight was typical of women domestics, for
whom the threat of rape, unwanted pregnancy, venereal
disease, victimisation or relegation to the fields was
ever-present.

Household servants and domestics are known to have posed
a serious discipline problem despite their precarious position.
They caused particular irritation to their white mistresses,
who accused them of pilfering, dishonesty, idleness, disobedience, negligence and, worst of all, forgetting their place.
Spelling out the problem as she saw it, Elizabeth Fenwick
described her hired help as belonging to

a sluggish, inert, self-willed race of people, apparently
inaccessible to gentle and kindly impulses. Nothing but

the dread of the whip seems capable of rousing them to exertion, & not even that can make them honest. Pilfering seems habitual and instinctive among domestic slaves.[10]

Writing a few years after Emancipation, Frances Lanaghan, a British woman who had lived in Antigua for many years, echoed these sentiments, complaining that her domestic servants

> think themselves upon an equality with the highest in the land . . . If you keep them at their proper distance, they become dissatisfied and complain of your being harsh to them, if, on the contrary, you shew them any degree of attention . . . they then assume too much and entirely forget the difference of rank. Try to serve them and it is ten chances to one that you make them your enemy; do them ninety-nine favours, and refuse the hundredth, and you are reviled and blamed as if you had injured them.[11]

Her contemporary, Mrs A. C. Carmichael, the wife of a Scottish planter who managed households in Trinidad and St Vincent in the 1820s, was especially incensed by the behaviour of the women who did her laundry. 'Of all your troublesome establishment', she ranted, 'the washerwomen are the most discontented, unmanageable and idle'. She described their wilful destruction of her clothes and house-hold linens as 'past belief'.[12] Even washing clothes, it seems, could be turned into a subtle act of sabotage.

The kind of behaviour she describes was by no means confined to domestic servants. Her reference to an enslaved woman who 'refused to do any useful work', but whose success as an entrepreneur enabled her to buy herself back from her owner, suggests that some women were single-minded in their determination to be rid of their shackles. In such a context, even everyday activities like growing and selling their own fruits and vegetables had the potential to be turned from a simple act of survival into a tool of quiet subversion. The profits from their activities would often be carefully squirrelled away over many years, their sole means of purchasing their own or their children's freedom. Meanwhile, the fact that such women could travel relatively freely to Sunday markets to sell their surplus produce provided a forum for them to meet, plan and exchange precious information.

There is no question, then, that some women simply put their foot down and refused to go along with the expect-ation that they should work themselves into the ground. Accused by planters and their agents as guilty of laziness or malingering, their actions were the modern-day equivalent of a go-slow – a form of individual resistance to any unacceptable work regime. London merchants Thomas and William King owned plantations in Grenada, Dominica and Demerara-Essequibo (later known as British Guiana). Their records, covering the two decades before slavery was abolished, refer to numerous women who were punished for this kind of insubordination. They include Henrietta, a female slave on the Friendship plantation, who was sentenced to a day and night in the stocks for 'continually omitting to comply with her task'; Quasheeba, who was punished for 'refusing to go to work when ordered by the doctor'; Clarissa, sentenced several times to solitary confinement for malingering and poor work; Lavinia, for 'abusive language' and 'leaving three fourths of her day's work unfinished'; and Caroline, for 'abusing the manager and overseer and defying the former to do his worst'.[13] Again, the threat of severe punishment was no deterrent.

The decision to escape was a more desperate act, though no less courageous. Consequences for runaways who were recaptured included savaging by dogs, amputation and, if their captors chose to make an example of them, torture and execution. Persistent offenders could expect to be clapped in leg or neck irons that severely restricted their mobility and prevented them from lying down to sleep. At best, they could expect a severe and very public flogging as a deterrent to anyone who might be harbouring thoughts of escape. The dangers described were well known, yet for people who had reached the end of their tether, it was apparently worth the risk. The desire to be free or escape brutal treatment motivated some runaways; for others, the prospect of seeing a lover, visiting a relative on another plantation or returning to the sanctuary of their family were incentive enough to abscond, sometimes for days or weeks.

In April 1829, planter Henry Marshall paid for an advertisement in the *Barbados Globe*, offering to reward anyone who would 'either apprehend and deliver to him or put in the slave prison, the slave Amelia, a yellow skin Negro girl, about 16 years old, with a Negro freckle under one of her eyes, an aperture in her top front teeth, and an excrescence behind each ear produced from them being pierced for rings'. Amelia had absconded the day after he'd purchased her, returning to her parents, Thomas and Harriet, who had hidden her away for three weeks before she was caught and returned. Undeterred by whatever punishment he gave her, Marshall complained that 'she has again absented herself since 30th November last . . . and is supposed to be harboured by her father and his connections'. His frustration at this young girl's audacity is almost audible.[14]

Although most women escaped alone, sometimes they took flight with others. Earlier that same year, slave-mistress Sarah Taylor had issued a warning in the local press against harbouring or employing three women runaways named Betty, Charlotte and Molly, threatening to enforce the law 'with the utmost rigour' should anyone try to assist them. Local newspapers were littered with such notices and shed an intriguing spotlight on the measures some women used to avoid capture. In 1817, when a woman named Chloe went missing, her owner warned that although born in Africa, her good command of English meant she could easily pass herself off as Creole. Two years later, when a woman named Nancy Effey fled with her two 'mulatto' children, her Bajan master (quite possibly the children's father) warned local constables to ignore any 'spurious papers' she might produce. It seems Nancy Effey had had the foresight to forge or steal the documents she would need when on the run. Another Bajan, a certain Mr E. S. White, whose slave woman Sarah went missing in June 1829, cautions 'all the masters of vessels against taking her from the island', suggesting that some women were even prepared to become ships' stowaways in their bid for freedom.

Women ran away less often than men and were also more likely to be caught, especially when they fled with children.

Yet in Grenada between 1808 and 1821, the number of females who absconded was on average twice as high as men.[15] Newspaper advertisements for runaways on the island include several references to women who absconded for years or decades at a time, often assuming false identities in an effort to disguise their status. There were also attempts like Sarah's, to flee overseas. Some women escaped with their children; others – in one case, a girl of only twelve years old – were little more than children themselves.

To escape was one thing, but to plot with others was a sin of a different order. To planters, whose nagging fear of insurrection was ever-present, rebellion was the absolute worst of all possible crimes. Attempts to establish the extent of women's involvement in slave revolts have been frustrated by a lack of surviving evidence and a tendency to focus on the handful of women who are said to have betrayed them. Accounts of planned rebellions in Antigua (1736), Monserrat (1768) and the armed uprising in Barbados (1816) all refer to women who acted as informers, yet there is no hard evidence that women were any more duplicitous than men. The fearsome methods used to extract information, and contemporary assumptions about women's frailty, suggests that they were probably the first to be tortured, regardless of whether they had anything useful to reveal.[16]

Even in Jamaica, where each new generation experienced the direct or indirect repercussions of a slave revolt, the role played by women is understated. The tendency is to focus on individual men and to describe their 'followers' as a genderless mob. But the fact that so few women are named as rebels does not mean they played no part.[17] In 1746, when a planned insurrection was uncovered in Antigua, just one of the forty-seven slaves put to death was a woman, yet it is clear that many more would have joined the rebels had the plan succeeded. A local councillor was struck by the women's insolence, convinced they 'had the utter Extirpation of the White as much at heart as the Men, and would undoubtedly have done as much mischief'.[18]

In an inquiry into the 1816 rebellion in Barbados, which resulted in the death of one white man and several hundred slaves, there were several reports of women who had become noticeably rude or subversive in the weeks leading up to the uprising. Some domestics had refused point-blank to take orders, others were less subtle. Planter Joseph Belgrave, in his evidence to the Barbados Assembly, referred to a black woman on the Carrington estate who had accosted and openly abused him, accusing him of being 'one of the fellows who prevented the slaves from having their freedom'. She went on to warn him that '(freedom) had been sent out for them, and they would have it'.[19]

Another witness, a slave called Robert, referred in his confession to a woman called Nanny Grigg on the Simmon plantation, an elderly domestic slave, who actively incited her fellow slaves to revolt. As he claimed:

Sometime the last year he heard the Negroes were all to be freed on New Year's Day. That Nanny Grigg, a Negro at Simmon's, who said she could read, was the first person who told the Negroes at Simmon's so; and she said she had read it in the Newspapers, and that her master was very uneasy at it; that she was always talking about it to the negroes and told them that they were all damned fools to work . . . That about a fortnight after New Year's Day, she said the negroes were to be freed on Easter Monday, and the only way to get it was to fight for it, otherwise they would not get it, and the way they were to do, was to set fire, as that was the way they did in St Domingo.[20]

There is no mention of obeah[21] in Robert's description, yet Nanny Grigg's role echoes that of the 'sage matrons' referred to in John Stedman's memoirs, whom he describes as 'a kind of Sibils, who deal in oracles'. According to Stedman, 'whatever the prophetess orders to be done . . . is most sacredly performed by the surrounding multitude, which renders these meetings extremely dangerous, as she frequently enjoins them to murder their masters or desert to the woods.'[22]

Stedman's account suggests that women were not only willing and active participants in slave insurrections but they may also, on some occasions, have been the instigators. Proof of the extent of their involvement is hidden away in surviving execution and deportation records, although much remains unearthed. Cubah, 'Queen of Kingston', is a rare and notable exception. In April 1760, many thousand Coromantee and Creole slaves, prompted by the threat of starvation and the severity of their conditions, took advantage of the diversion of British imperial forces in the Seven Years War and rose up simultaneously throughout St Mary's parish in Jamaica. They set sugar works and cane fields alight, gathering recruits of both sexes as they went. At Heywood Hall, the 'mulatto' mistress of the slain overseer was raped, but her life was apparently spared at the intercession of slaves from a neighbouring estate, who (contrary to the popular stereotype of the treacherous concubine) considered her to be 'on *their* side'.[23] Two months later, it was clear that 'Tacky's Rebellion' had not been contained when a plot was uncovered in Kingston:

> It was discovered that the Coromantins of that town had raised one Cubah, a female slave belonging to a Jewess, to the rank of Royalty and dubbed her 'Queen of Kingston'; at their meetings she had sat in state under a canopy, with a sort of robe on her shoulders and a crown upon her head.[24]

Although Cubah's precise role in Tacky's Rebellion is undocumented, there seems little doubt that she was in the vanguard of the rebellion. She was certainly more than a flamboyant figurehead whose sole purpose was to rally the troops. From her description, she seems to have been elevated to a distinct traditional role, similar to that of the queen mother of the Ashanti. That Cubah was fully committed to the rebellion is confirmed by Edward Long himself. He described how, when seized and deported, 'she prevailed upon the Captain . . . to put her ashore again on the Leeward part of the island',[25] from where she is known to have rejoined the rebels. It took several months before she was finally recaptured and executed.

The anonymous Cubahs and Nanny Griggs who played similar roles in other slave rebellions are rarely acknow-ledged. Contemporary eyewitnesses, invariably male, have tended to focus on the part played by male figureheads like Tacky and Sam Sharpe. Yet as the number of transported

Africans decreased and the population came to consist of more and more people who had been born into slavery, the role women played in slave revolts seems to have evolved. Both planters and fellow slaves accused women of verbal sedition and incitement to riot. Women are also known to have acted as go-betweens, liaising with Maroons or rebel slaves. They were evidently prepared to risk their lives, for they were sent to the gallows for their involvement just like men were, often after enduring unimaginable torture.

Bernard Senior's account of the Christmas Rebellion in Jamaica in 1831–1832, during which he led a number of military sorties against insurgent slaves, mentions several women who wilfully concealed information, including a woman who led his party straight into a rebel ambush. Another woman had been seized while acting as a guide for a rebel foraging party. She was allegedly chosen for this task because of her acquaintance with the slaves' provision grounds in the area.[26] Although such references to women are sparse, they suggest that the mobility women enjoyed when carrying out their marketing activities and cultivating their provision grounds rendered them almost invisible, giving them a distinct advantage as spies, messengers or guides.[27]

When outright rebellion was not possible, women found other ways to disrupt or undermine their owners' intent. Some were even prepared to kill their tormentors and pay the ultimate price. In the 1730s, a rector was duped by one of his parishioners, 'a Black Woman . . . well instructed in our Religion . . . [who] had not long been arrived at Nevis, before she poisoned four White Persons, and was executed for so doing'.[28] In 1753, the local assembly in St Kitts was informed that a female slave named Baby had been executed for the murder of her owner, a Mr Thomas Barnaby.[29] There are many more examples.

Monk Lewis referred several times in his diary to female poisoners who exploited their position as cooks and a house servant in order to make attempts on their owners' lives. The death of Mr Forbes, a neighbouring planter, was apparently the result of his having been 'poisoned with a corrosive sublimate by a female slave who was executed in consequence'.[30] Another neighbour, he wrote,

> had three (domestics) in prison . . . one of them grown grey in his service, for poisoning him . . . his brother was actually killed by similar means. Another agent . . . was obliged to quit an estate from the frequent attempts to poison him; and a person against whom there is no sort of charge alleged for tyranny, after being brought to the doors of death by a cup of coffee, only escaped a second time by his civility in giving the beverage, prepared for himself, to two young book-keepers, to both of whom it proved fatal. It indeed came out afterwards that this crime was also effected by the abominable belief in Obeah.[31]

The woman who prepared this fatal draught subsequently claimed that she had 'no idea of its being poison', insisting that she had been advised by the obeah man that it would merely act as 'a charm to make her massah good to her'.

Women like this, who could present attempted murder as an act of humble flattery, must have been legion. Their

elusive presence in the surviving records hints at the existence of a Quasheeba who was every bit as sharp-witted and
manipulative as Quashee, her obsequious, hand-wringing
partner in crime.[32] But while Quasheeba's skills of decep-
tion may have equalled his, her powers of perception and
her insight into the psyche of her tormentors must have
been in a class of their own. As both nanny and wet nurse,
she was the surrogate mother of both her future owner and
his offspring, enjoying an intimate if subordinate rapport
with these children that even their natural mothers must
have envied. As her master's first sexual conquest and subsequent bed warmer, she may also have become his most
intimate confidante. No wonder women in this situation
sometimes took advantage of their position when opportunities arose to secure preferential treatment.

One such woman is Old Doll, who, together with her
three daughters, a sister and a niece, manipulated her role as
housekeeper on the Newton plantation in Barbados for over
fifty years. Old Doll and her family of women achieved
such an elevated status in the household that they acquired
slaves of their own to perform their designated chores. The
fact that they did so little work themselves gave the estate
manager, Sampson Wood, a serious headache. In his report
to Newton's owner in 1796, he claimed that the daughters
were 'young strong, healthy and have never done anything',
adding that they had been so thoroughly spoilt that hard
work 'would kill them at once'.

By his own admission, this was not entirely accurate, for
an earlier attempt to punish them by putting them to work
as field hands had obviously backfired. They were 'absolutely
a nuisance in the field and set the worst of examples to the

rest of the negroes' – to the extent that they were returned to the house and given occasional needlework to do. These women clearly had an escape plan. Today we would condemn it as colourism, but for them it probably made perfect sense. By confining their relationships to white men, they made sure that they and their children would eventually pass for white and thus gain their freedom.[33]

Somehow Old Doll and her relatives acquired a stake in the system, and they milked it to the full. Others in her position – women like Nanny Grigg, for example – exploited their domestic status to undermine it, using their access to information to educate themselves and apprise their fellow sufferers. Maria Nugent, wife of a Jamaican governor who shared the paranoia of her fellow planters, was under no allusion about the dangers of careless talk. Referring to the successful slave rebellion in Haiti, which had left slave owners across the Caribbean quaking in their boots, she remarked:

> The splendour of the black chiefs of Santo Domingo, their superior strength, their firmness of character . . . are common topics at dinner; and the blackies in attendance seem so much interested, that they hardly change a plate or do anything but listen.[34]

Women such as these were much more than a product of sexual or domestic intimacy. Like Cubah, Minelta, Mary Anne, Jenny and their countless anonymous sisters, they possessed far deeper resources than those for which they've been given credit. The most powerful and enduring of these was their role as the primary conveyors of culture. This meant clinging to their belief in the medicinal powers of plants; adhering to remembered birthing and weaning practices; adapting their song, dances, dress and food preparation; and reviving their traditional leadership roles. By passing this knowledge on to each new generation, these women ensured that Africa's lost children would not only retain their cultural identity but survive to tell the tale.

Enslaved woman and child

6

Choice or Circumstance?
Slave Women and Reproduction

I really believe that the Negresses can produce children at
pleasure; and where they are barren, it is just as hens will
frequently not lay eggs on shipboard because they do not like
the situation.
      Monk Lewis, Jamaican slave owner, London, 1845

If their experience of physical and sexual abuse gave women
an added incentive to resist enslavement, their assigned
roles – which were also determined by their gender – gave
them some unique opportunities to subvert it. Nowhere is
this more apparent than in the evidence surrounding their
poor reproductive performance. Across the Caribbean, as
planters grew increasingly anxious to replenish the slave-
force from their existing 'stock', the issue of women's
fertility became *the* number one talking point. Black women
simply weren't breeding fast enough, and theories abounded
as to why.

In 1807, the year Parliament finally voted to put an end to the transatlantic slave trade, there were an estimated 775,000 slaves in the British West Indies. By 1834, the year slaves were supposedly freed, the population had fallen to 665,000.[1] In Jamaica, there was a decline of around 12 per cent of the enslaved population in less than thirty years.[2] The most obvious causes have been explored in earlier chapters and were clearly beyond women's control – delayed or absent menstruation, premature menopause, sterility and all the other gynaecological consequences of the punishing regime. That these harsh conditions contributed to the rapidly declining birth rate is indisputable. Even so, there is evidence that some enslaved women made *a conscious decision* to limit or control their own fertility. In doing so, they were exercising one of the few subjective choices available to them to strike at the very heart of the plantation system.

From the earliest period of settlement, birth rates on Britain's West Indian sugar colonies were abysmal. The gender imbalance among so-called 'saltwater negroes', typically more men than women in the early years, was partly to blame. As mentioned, this imbalance was not consistent across all islands or plantations. Nevertheless, with the exception of Barbados, imported African women are known to have been outnumbered by as many as three to one on certain ships, and on some Jamaican estates, the male-to-female ratio is said to have been even higher. As well as the exacting workload and semi-starvation diet, the lack of opportunities for any kind of normal, social life was another contributing factor, reflecting the popular view prior to Abolition that it was 'better to buy than breed'.

As more people were born into slavery, women's life expectancy did improve. But as they grew more resilient, the rate of natural decrease in the population should have, in theory, slowed down. In fact, though, it plummeted, causing growing alarm among members of the West India Lobby, whose excessive profits and lavish lifestyles were wholly dependent on maintaining their stock of slaves.

Toward the end of the eighteenth century, with the possibility of abolition looming, many slaveholders attempted to follow Barbados's example. There, half a century earlier, the dwindling slave population had prompted such dismay that planters had introduced a number of bold new incentives to encourage more women to breed. As well as upping the number of females imported from Africa to address the gender imbalance, labour hours were reduced for pregnant and breastfeeding women. Local planters were also urged to relax social and travel constraints, to allow more opportunities for slaves to procreate naturally. Though frowned upon elsewhere, as early as the 1770s, dances and other social gatherings had become a part of social life on Bajan plantations. Apparently, it was not uncommon to see 'both sexes . . . frequently travelling all night, going to or coming from a distant connection, without sleep, to be in due time to go through a hard day's labour, after their nocturnal adventures'.[3]

Financial perks were on offer, too. As well as being given lighter duties, mothers of young babies were offered cash rewards for 'bringing out a child'. Accounts from the Mount Gay and Newton estates show that women who gave birth around the end of the eighteenth century could expect to receive just over six shillings if their child survived the first nine days of life, when lockjaw and other complications were most likely to set in. Midwives were also given a bonus for each live birth. It was only when these measures failed to work that managers like Samson Wood on the Newton estate began to suspect something else was afoot. Writing to his employer in 1797, his frustration was barely concealed: 'I am very sorry our Negroes have decreased this year', he lamented. 'I know not how it has happened for they have had great care taken of them and have wanted for nothing. The women have been unsuccessful generally in breeding and childbirth.'[4]

Given what we know about their circumstances, 'the women have been unsuccessful' is an interesting turn of phrase. It's almost as if, despite their grim conditions, the women were seen as somehow to blame for their own infertility. There was much speculation about what they might be up to. Clutching at straws (and typical of European attitudes toward the dangers of bathing at the time), William Dickson thought it might have something to do with the women's attempts to keep themselves clean: 'Most of the black women are very subject to obstructions, from what cause I will not presume to say; but perhaps they may be ascribed in part, to their using restringent baths or washing themselves in cool water at improper periods.' He also blamed 'the absurd management of Negro midwives', whose birthing practices were thought to be particularly harmful. Apparently, the possibility that a high proportion of women might simply be sterile was not something he considered.[5]

Eventually, the birth rate on Barbados did start to improve. But while the island's planters congratulated themselves for being ahead of the game, their counterparts in Grenada, Tobago, Jamaica and elsewhere were growing increasingly desperate. To boost slave numbers, many resorted to illegal imports of captive Africans purchased from the Spanish, prompting Parliament to insist that a detailed register of slaves be kept on every estate onward from 1812.

Well before abolition threatened to cut off fresh supplies from Africa, planters' journals and correspondence are full of laments about the difficulties they were encountering in their efforts to reverse their dwindling slave stocks. The surviving evidence only hints at the extent of women's intransigence, yet as early as 1746, Jamaican governor Edward Trelawny claimed that 'what chiefly contributes to there being so few children among the English Negroes is the practice of wenches in procuring abortions'.[6]

Estate inventories suggest that his suspicions were well founded. Records from Jamaica's Mesopotamia plantation show that of 200 women of childbearing age who lived there between 1799 and 1828, at least half bore no live children. In fact, over a period of almost thirty years, there were around seventy-five potential mothers living on the estate at any one time, yet on average they produced only six live births annually between them.[7]

Similarly, on the Worthy Park estate, the average birth rate in 1793 was under twenty per thousand. According to the calculations of its owner, out of 240 women, only eighty-nine had actually given birth, and of these just nineteen had a child that survived.[8] A similar situation was to be found on many other islands, particularly on sugar plantations where conditions were notoriously harsh. Neither African nor island-born women were reproducing, although Creole women were marginally more fertile, as were women who worked in the animal pens or the great house, where the labour regime was said to be less exacting.

On Martinique, Saint-Domingue and other islands in the French Antilles, planters faced the same dilemma. There were loud and anxious calls for the legislature to concentrate on 'the increase by reproduction of the agricultural population whose maintenance is indispensable to the existence of the colonies'.[9] There, too, the survival of the plantation economy was placed firmly on the shoulders of enslaved women. Indeed, they were held liable to such an extent that a slave owner in Saint-Domingue ordered his overseer to whip both mother and midwife whenever a child died at birth. Perversely, he also had unsuccessful mothers placed in neck irons until they fell pregnant again, although how he expected them to conceive when so constrained remains a mystery.[10]

As the birth rate continued to fall, planters and abolitionists argued at length about the whys and wherefores, with the latter insisting that the incidence of 'degrading, disgusting and depopulating promiscuous intercourse' in the slaves' quarters could only be addressed by giving them Christian instruction.[11] The issue was so topical that in 1789 and 1790, opponents and supporters of slavery debated the possible causes before the Privy and Select Committees of the House of Commons.

To divert attention from allegations of neglect and physical abuse, pro-slavers were quick to point the finger. The decline in slave numbers, they insisted, was largely beyond their control. Among other things, they blamed extended weaning, maternal neglect, 'barbaric' mating patterns, African childbirth customs, incest, venereal diseases, male debility resulting from 'over-indulgence in spirituous liquors', female promiscuity and the taking of 'specifics to cause abortion'.[12]

Blaming the victims was all the rage. Whatever their pet theories, the key witnesses – planters, doctors, representatives of island assemblies and other contemporary observers, all of them white and male – insisted that enslaved men and women were at the root of the problem. Reverend Thomas Malthus condemned 'promiscuous intercourse, unnatural passions, violations of the marriage bed and improper arts to conceal the consequences of irregular connections'. A representative of the Jamaican Assembly spoke of 'foul acts of sensuality and intemperance'. Others spoke of 'a shocking licentiousness and profligacy of the spirit caused by the practice of polygamy' or alluded to 'obeah arts' and 'witchcraft'. Their biased testimony is a perfect example of how pseudo-scientific racism, so rampant in nineteenth-century Britain, was used to downplay slave owners' responsibility and justify the economic imperatives of the day.

Given planters' treatment of enslaved women, their hypocrisy beggars belief. The 'venereal taint', a consequence of the slaves' latent immorality, was a major cause of women's poor fertility, they argued, not helped by a tendency to regard the young as 'an encumbrance to their nocturnal meetings and dances'.[13] Meanwhile, humanitarians and religious reformers pounced on such theories, using them to argue the case for marriage and active missionary intervention. Yet the notion that moral reform would be an incentive for enslaved women to give birth proved overly optimistic.

Many of the arguments put forward during these parliamentary hearings are easy to discount, especially with the benefit of historical hindsight. For example, there is no evidence to suggest that women's fertility has suffered in African societies where polygamy, prolonged weaning and postnatal sexual abstinence continue to be practised. Indeed, a few years earlier, colonial administrator Edward Long had argued that the practice of polygamy in West Africa 'contributes greatly to populousness'.[14] Nor does the theory that venereal diseases impaired women's fertility explain the comparatively high birth rates within European populations at the time, where gonorrhoea and syphilis were just as prevalent, possibly in a more virulent form. The view that infants were regarded as an inconvenience is equally suspect. Motherhood was seen as the height of a woman's achievement in most African societies and there are countless references to the fierce and enduring bonds that existed between enslaved women and their offspring, especially in situations where mothers witnessed their children being 'sold away'.

As the drive to improve slave fertility became increasingly linked to planters' very survival, legislation was adopted throughout the British sugar colonies, heralding a new era of 'pro-natalism'. For a rare moment in history, black women were actively encouraged to have babies and plenty of them. As an added incentive, the Jamaican Assembly passed an act in 1788 entitling overseers to twenty shillings for every newborn who survived the first two weeks of life, and offering planters a tax remission for the same amount. The Consolidated Slave Act of 1792 increased this sum to three pounds and made women with more than six children exempt from labour. By 1799, Whitehall was instructing planters to offer monetary incentives to parents and midwives, along with extra food rations and a six-to-eight week exemption from labour both before and after delivery for all slave mothers. Seen from afar, enslaved pregnant women had never had it so good.

On some estates, their diet was improved and corporal punishment reduced to confinement in the stocks. Elsewhere, baptism and marriage were introduced in an attempt to curb the practice of 'obeah arts' and encourage monogamy. Inspired by the example of Barbados, many planters built lying-in hospitals, in which better-trained midwives could supervise births. The hope was that African childbirth customs, thought to be especially dangerous, could be more strictly controlled. This practice became compulsory in 1798, when the Amelioration Act required every plantation to make provisions for a 'commodious' hospital and a twice-weekly visit from a doctor, tasked with giving special attention to pregnant women and their newborns. In Jamaica alone, between 1791 and 1795, more than fifty new doctors were employed, at least half of them Scottish or Irish. But the proverbial horse had already bolted, and a decade after abolition, despite all these measures, the population continued to spiral downward.

A few planters met with limited success, but local census records, now mandatory, confirm that most were unable to reverse this plunging trend. Officially, imports from Africa ceased in 1807, by which time women were beginning to outnumber men on most large sugar estates, yet the evidence speaks for itself: Between 1815 and 1819, St Lucia recorded a population decrease of 25.5 per cent. Likewise, between 1819 and 1821, Tobago saw its population plummet by 26 per cent. In Grenada between 1817 and 1819, there was a decline of 18 per cent. In Jamaica, the decrease went from 0.7 per 1,000 to 4.8 per 1,000 in the span of just sixteen years.[15] With the exception of Barbados, no single island in the British West Indies achieved a meaningful increase in its slave population much before 1832.[16] By way of contrast, on the American mainland, where imports from Africa were also officially banned, the slave population had increased tenfold. Even the harsh excesses of sugar cultivation could not account for such a huge discrepancy.

Resistance by planters and their agents may have been partly to blame. Despite all the public hand-wringing, few plantation managers embraced these reforms wholeheartedly, if only because of the drain on their finances. In a context of widespread absenteeism, the men responsible for the daily management of the plantation found themselves caught in a double bind. On the one hand, they were under mounting pressure from their absent employers to increase profits by exacting more labour from the slaveforce. On the other, they were expected to respond to growing political pressure to improve the slaves' conditions. Forced to squeeze profits from increasingly uneconomical estates, many estate managers would have simply ignored Whitehall's edicts and carried on as usual. After all, most owners were thousands of miles away and had never set foot on a West Indian plantation. They could easily claim ignorance if their managers and overseers stepped up the physical abuse in their quest for bigger returns.[17]

Members of the anti-slavery lobby certainly thought so. In their view, the reforms were ineffective due to the continuing impact of poor diet and coercive labour conditions.[18] Records from the York and Worthy Park estates in Jamaica appear to support this view. On both plantations in the years leading up to Emancipation, female slaves came to make up a larger proportion of the field gangs, with disastrous consequences for their health.[19] Indeed, as earlier chapters have shown, evidence that women came to perform an increasingly disproportionate share of the most debilitating work is to be found on all West Indian sugar colonies – at a time, incidentally, when pregnant white women were discouraged from even so much as bending down to open a drawer.

The physical consequences of such a punishing work regime have already been quantified, but in the absence of testimony from the women themselves, the psychological effects can only be guessed. Nevertheless, there are some intriguing clues. Repeated references by planters and their agents to the women's 'refusal' to breed hint at a long-standing aversion to the idea of bringing children into bondage, despite the revered status of mothers. In 1809, for example, Jamaican attorney Webb informed the absentee owner of Mesopotamia that 'every inducement that can be devised has been held out in order to encourage the women to breed'. Two years later, he was still lamenting the island-wide decrease, claiming that 'by far the greater proportion [of plantations] are on the reverse side'. The following year, if his account is to be believed, he introduced further incentives in the form of a cow or a hog for every new mother. According to him, 'the women's not breeding is neither owing to their being hard worked or in any respect badly treated . . . there are no Negroes in the Parish of Westmoreland who are better indulged, better fed or better clothed'.[20] Attorney John Shand echoed his concerns. In 1814, he wrote to inform the heir to Lord Penryn's Jamaica estate that, despite persistent efforts to induce the slave women to breed, 'the balance does not turn the other way and we cannot boast a regular increase, however small'.[21]

Unlike these men, planter Monk Lewis, who had a reputation locally for being too soft on his slaves, had little incentive to exaggerate his humanitarian response to the problem. On his first visit to Jamaica in 1816, he describes how he introduced better food for pregnant women, special care for nursing mothers and a dollar reward for every mother and midwife who safely delivered a child. Yet on his return to the estate in 1818, he found that 'among upwards of 330 Negroes and with a greater number of females than men, in spite of all indulgences and inducements, not more than twelve or thirteen children have been added annually to the lists'.[22] Moreover, out of a female slave population of more than 150, only eight women were 'on the breeding list'. Something was clearly afoot.

The exploitation of their children's labour and the callous separation of infants from their mothers were probably incentive enough for enslaved women to avoid giving birth if they could. In Jamaica, as elsewhere, the separation of slave families was not forbidden in law until 1826. Until then, children could be sold or given away 'like puppies from a litter'. Despite the prospect of a financial reward for giving birth, many women found that pregnancy and motherhood afforded them no special treatment. Mary Prince's account of the abuse of a pregnant woman called Hetty bears witness to this fact:

> Poor Hetty, my fellow slave, was very kind to me, and I used to call her my Aunt; but she led a most miserable life, and her death was hastened (at least the slaves all believed and said so,) by the dreadful chastisement she received from my master during her pregnancy. It happened as follows. One of the cows had dragged the rope away from the stake to which Hetty had fastened it, and got loose. My master flew into a terrible passion and ordered the poor creature to be stripped quite naked, notwithstanding her pregnancy, and to be tied up to a tree in the yard. He then flogged her as hard as he could lick, both with the whip and cow-skin, till she was all over streaming, with blood. He rested, and then beat her again and again. Her shrieks were terrible, the consequence was that poor Hetty was brought to bed before her time and was delivered after severe labour of a dead child. She appeared to recover after her confinement, so far that she was repeatedly flogged by both master and mistress afterwards; but her former strength never returned to her. Ere long her body and limbs swelled to a great size; and she lay on a mat in the kitchen, till the water burst out of her body and she died. All the slaves said that death was a good thing for poor Hetty; but I cried very much for her death. The manner of it filled me with horror.[23]

As we have seen from earlier accounts, Hetty's fate, though extreme, was by no means unusual. She was one of thousands of nameless women whose pregnancies were brought to an abrupt end because of an overly enthusiastic flogging or persistent physical abuse. Yet the act of bringing a child into the world who, from the moment of their birth, would be classified as someone else's property, represented more-than-guaranteed personal suffering. To increase their owner's stock was to enhance his wealth and boost his long-term prosperity. For women with no stake in the system's survival, this would have made no sense whatsoever.

African women may have been naked on arrival, but part of the cultural 'baggage' that they brought with them to the Americas was their knowledge of preventative and curative medicines. Women played a vital role as healers and mystics in most African societies, and many would have known which plants could be used to induce a miscarriage. Despite planters' efforts to repress such practices, they continued undercover. Some have even argued that they thrived. A 1970s study of Mammy Forbes, the Jamaican healer and 'doctoress', which compared her practice with that of Nana Oparebea, queen mother of the Ohemma Ku society in Ghana, concluded that their methods were uncannily similar, so much so that the author was 'amazed at the purity with which the African tradition has apparently been retained in Jamaica, despite the rigour of slavery'.[24]

Given the woefully inadequate healthcare they received, there was plenty of scope for the enslaved to pursue African medical practices. As well as being more accessible, they were quite likely preferred to the dubious benefits of being confined to plantation 'hot-houses', where European doctors were known for their over-reliance on bleeding and purging. Detailed knowledge of the properties of herbs, roots, barks and plants, passed through generations, meant there were always women who could offer a range of treatments and remedies for common ailments, including, among other things, laxatives, sedatives, antidiarrhoeals, inoculations and abortifacients.

Edward Long was particularly impressed by the effectiveness of African herbal medicines, describing them as 'wonderfully powerful'. In fact, he claimed they 'subdued diseases incident to their climate which have foiled the art of European surgeons'.[25] Evidently, enslaved women knew how to prevent childbirth if they wished to. That some took advantage of this option is suggested by the planters and doctors themselves, who frequently denounced them for inducing miscarriages and abortions in order to be free to carry on their 'licentious' sex lives.

Testifying in 1790, Dr Robert Thomas informed the House of Commons Select Committee that the continuing decrease in slave numbers in the sugar colonies was in part due to 'the frequent abortions which Negro women designedly bring on themselves, either because a state of pregnancy in some measure puts a stop to their amorous pursuits . . . or because they do not choose to be encumbered with the trouble of giving suck and of rearing children'.[26] Jamaican practitioner Dr Michael Clare, in evidence to a later committee, claimed that midwives were known to administer wild cassava to women seeking abortion, which he described as 'a drastic of the most violent kind'.[27]

Like the measures taken to avoid conception, the extent of abortion is impossible to gauge, for it was a practice that planters and overseers could not possibly control. The wilful termination of a pregnancy was by definition a private and surreptitious act which, provided there were no obvious medical consequences, went largely unrecorded. Calculated at around one in every 4.6 live births at the Worthy Park estate in Jamaica, even such a high number of miscarriages can only hint at the agency of women. Without doubt, there were many who shunned such drastic measures. Nevertheless, the frustrated attempts of planters and their agents to encourage a self-generating workforce suggest a level of sabotage they were helpless to contain.

Given the extreme and degrading circumstances with which women were confronted, even infanticide could be seen as a subversive act in some cases. Newborn babies were especially vulnerable to disease, neglect and infection, so the mothers' motives or complicity are hard to second-guess. After a lifetime of brutality, the mindset of enslaved women would have been unsentimental. In fact, smothering a child might well have been regarded by some as a mercy killing. In Saint-Domingue, a midwife who confessed to murdering seventy newborns was unrepentant when her crime was uncovered. 'See if I deserve death!' she is said to have exclaimed. 'It is a shameful custom to raise children into slavery'. On the same island, an enslaved woman accused of murdering both of her children expressed similar sentiments. Her desire, she said, was to 'steal them away from slavery'.[28]

This reluctance to bring children into slavery is supported by more empirical evidence. Planters were especially put out by the habit of lengthy weaning, for example, yet their records show that most slave mothers insisted on nursing their children for a minimum of two or three years. Young mothers would have relied on other women for advice in such matters. They would have known that prolonged breastfeeding was believed to afford them a degree of contraceptive protection, enabling them to space out their pregnancies in defiance of their owners' efforts to entice them to breed more frequently.

The belief that breastfeeding would delay reconception had a cultural basis. The West African custom of avoiding intercourse whilst breastfeeding is thought to have been widely practised in the slave quarters. Polygamous relationships, in which men acquired several 'wives' or long-term partners, relieved new mothers of their sexual obligations since men were expected to sleep with their other women while a woman was breastfeeding her child. John Stedman, who spent some years in Surinam, observed that 'during the two years which [the women] continue to suckle, they never cohabit with their husbands; this is considered unnatural and prejudicial to the infants'.[29]

That delayed weaning was a conscious contraceptive choice is also confirmed by the experience of Jamaican planter John Baillee, whose attempts to induce women to reduce the nursing period also met with dismal failure. In 1808, he offered two dollars to every mother who weaned her child within twelve months of delivery; however, his records reveal that *not a single mother availed herself of the premium* between 1808 and 1832.[30] It seems likely that, by the time pro-natalist policies were introduced during the final decades of slavery, women were already hardened to the idea of breeding for 'massah'. Put another way, a partial

alleviation of their suffering that stopped short of unconditional freedom was simply not acceptable.

Whether these women were aware that their actions
threatened the very fabric of slavery is impossible to say.
They would certainly have known that any child born to an
enslaved mother, whatever the colour or status of the father,
was automatically classified a slave. By taking steps to avoid
conception, space out their pregnancies or reject motherhood altogether, they were at very least contributing to a
general climate of non-cooperation. Unlike other subversive
acts they may have contemplated, abortion, infanticide and
the use of contraceptive devices were choices that afforded
women a degree of self-determination, something their
owners had no power to control. Their options may have
been few, but in all spheres of their existence, enslaved
women appear to have exploited to the full any opportunity
to give their lives meaning and agency.

This recalcitrant attitude is implied in the words of
Sabrina Park, a slave mother who was tried and convicted
for the murder of her three-month-old child. As she testified
in the court records, she had 'worked enough for buckra
already and would not be plagued to raise the child to work
for white people'. Monk Lewis, who witnessed the trial,
suggested that Sabrina was slightly mad; but a more sympathetic view of her predicament points to a different
conclusion. Drastic as it may sound, in the context of
West Indian slavery – and also of slavery in the American
South, where disproportionate incidents of the smothering
or 'overlaying' of newborns were reported – resorting to
abortion or infanticide may have been one of the most
effective weapons these desperate mothers possessed.[31]

Predictably, as the prospect of emancipation became a genuine possibility, some enslaved populations began to show an increase. In St Kitts between 1831 and 1834, the population grew by 4.6 per cent. In Monserrat between 1828 and 1831, there was a growth of 9.5 per cent. Similar increases were witnessed on Dominica and several other islands. It's almost as if the women, sensing that freedom was just around the corner, decided it was safe at last to give birth.

The most persuasive evidence that this refusal to breed may have been an act of conscious or subconscious resistance comes from Jamaica, where the steady recovery of the black population in the years following Emancipation was nothing short of remarkable. From an average of 28.4 per 1,000 in the period between 1817 and 1829, the birth rate in Jamaica began to rise in the mid-1830s and was approaching 40 per 1,000 by 1840.[32] This happened despite the sudden exodus of European doctors, the closure of plantation hospitals and the dire social and economic conditions that were among slavery's legacy.

Planter Monk Lewis expressed a rare insight into the capacity of obstinate women to defend their reproductive autonomy when he wrote in his journal:

I really believe that the Negresses can produce children at pleasure, and where they are barren it is just as hens will frequently not lay eggs on shipboard, because they do not like their situation.[33]

Sugar cane cutters, Jamaica, circa 1905

7

The Carriers of Roots:
Women and Culture

In this great future, you can't forget your past
So dry your tears, I say
No woman, no cry . . .

Bob Marley, 1975

At the root of enslaved women's stubborn refusal to bow down and accept their lot was an attitude that, to a greater or lesser extent, permeated the slave quarters on every island. Expressed in myriad ways, both active and passive, it can be summed up in one word: *resistance.*

Planters and their agents regarded this subversive mindset as a major threat to stability and responded with harsh, oppressive policies that they defended to the last. Yet to the enslaved it would have been a source of hope and empowerment. Their actions show that their opposition to slavery was not just a rejection of their status as human chattel. It is also an expression of their desire for unconditional freedom, a subtle-yet-powerful affirmation of their right to a self-determined life.[1]

One way of asserting this sense of agency was by adhering to African cultures, values and belief systems. In practice (and among other things), this meant clinging to their knowledge of the medicinal powers of plants; following remembered birthing and weaning practices; adapting stories, musical instruments and festivals; and reinventing traditional leadership roles. By passing this collective wisdom on to each new generation, enslaved women were able to mount a concerted and enduring defence against their owners' daily assaults on their humanity.

Slaveholders' efforts to suppress these cultural 'weapons' proved futile, not least because they were constantly reinforced by new arrivals from Africa. Planters knew from bitter experience that the presence of 'saltwater negroes' in the slave quarters could incite revolt, and some were reluctant to import fresh labour from Africa for this very reason. Their fear of the rallying power of African languages and rituals often led to excessive efforts to repress them.

Their paranoia was so great that on many plantations it was an offence for slaves to meet together in large numbers, while drumming or speaking in African tongues could be punishable by death. For isolated planters, hopelessly outnumbered and only too aware of their precarious position, even the imitation of things African was seen as a threat. However subtle, such expressions of cultural autonomy would have been an unsettling reminder that the people they had tried so hard to dehumanise were capable of rising above their abject circumstances to celebrate life on their own terms.

Having arrived naked and traumatised, their ability to rally, adapt and exploit their inner resources is nothing short of phenomenal. Fuelled by its own cultural dynamism, each embryonic nation would become a unique melting pot of people from widely different social, religious and cultural backgrounds. The Caribs, Arawaks and other original inhabitants of the islands who had escaped the Europeans' systematic extermination in the early days of settlement are known to have joined forces with Maroons or set up homes with enslaved women, adding their own unique footprint into the mix. The result was a novel blend of African cultures and languages with those of the different European settlers and the few surviving indigenous peoples who had not been wiped out.

Faced with such a confusing diversity of influences, the challenges of sustaining a distinctly non-European identity from one generation to the next must have been huge. Until abolitionist arguments for religious reform unleashed a growing army of missionaries, ignorance and illiteracy were the default. The prevailing diet of racist European propaganda, which vilified all things African, would have been easily swallowed. It was a systematic effort to alienate enslaved peoples from their roots and promote a dumbed-down, slave mentality, and clearly some individuals succumbed. Those who did not probably had a woman to thank.

As the bearers and carers of children, women played a crucial role in keeping alive the memory of who they once were. As cooks, lovers, grandmothers, surrogates and nursemaids, their influence spread, reaching into every crevice and corner of the slave quarters. Their practical tools included dress, language, hair and food preparation, singing, dancing, and a multitude of other ways of expressing their sense of self and community. With so little leisure time, this must have been hard to sustain. Nevertheless, women played a key role in defining the precious little free time available, which revolved around activities such as cooking and storytelling, typically in communal yards.

Even the smallest of freedoms were exploited to this end. The sale or barter of foodstuffs and other goods, for example, fulfilled a desire for economic independence that West Africa's market women have demonstrated for centuries. Drawing from their collective memory of the life they'd been forced to abandon, many enslaved women became skilled marketeers or 'higglers', hoarding the small profits they made from selling their own and others' produce at Sunday markets. Some used the money to purchase necessities or extra food; others, as we've seen, had longer-term plans.

Ironically, the strength of these cultural influences was an unintended consequence of slaveholders' own stereotypes. During the early period of settlement in Jamaica, many of the island's planters expressed a distinct preference for 'Coromantees'. In practice, this meant that for successive generations of Jamaicans, Fante-Akan culture was the foundation on which they built. Planter Bryan Edwards, who published a history of the British West Indies in 1801, was remarkably complimentary about their qualities, claiming that

> The circumstances which distinguish the Koromantyn, or Gold Coast, Negroes, from all others are firmness both of body and mind; a ferociousness of disposition; but withal, activity, courage, and a stubbornness, or what

an ancient Roman would have deemed an elevation of soul, which prompts them to enterprises of difficulty and danger; and enables them to meet death, in its most horrible shape, with fortitude or indifference.[2]

Views like this had a knock-on effect on the slave market, so much so that modern Ghana, known to slavers as the Gold Coast, supplied a quarter of all Jamaica's slave imports between 1655 and 1730 and a third between 1730 and 1790.

Consequently, everyday words as well as practices, values and belief systems retained distinct Fante-Akan overtones, providing a way of relating to others, interpreting the world, celebrating the life cycle and giving expression to people's hopes and fears. And because this culture was a vital, changing phenomenon, something that could be moulded to accommodate other cultural influences and adapted to meet the changing demands of plantation life, it survived and endured despite planters' efforts to stamp out all identification with Africa. Terms like *ebruni* (or *oburoni*), the Fante word for 'stranger' or 'foreigner' (literally 'those who come from over the horizon') are still used in Maroon communities to this day, evidence of its extraordinary cultural staying power.

In the words of one historian, Akan culture became 'a focus and symbol of resistance in Jamaica [that was] almost normative'.[3] Its terms of reference included deference to women, a long-standing reputation for female military prowess and communal survival strategies in which women played an active, sometimes central role.

Nowhere is this more evident than in the legendary reputation of Nanny the Maroon. Her practical and inspirational roles were grounded firmly in the tradition of the Ashanti warrior-priestess, and like Yaa Asentwaa, her function in battle was to provide both spiritual and tactical guidance. Nanny directed and spiritually sustained the guerrilla forces in the Blue Mountain area during the First Maroon War of 1733–1739. Surviving legends speak of her uncompromising bravery when facing the enemy and her awesome powers as an obeah woman. She is said to have kept a huge cauldron, which boiled without the aid of fire, into which unsuspecting British soldiers were lured to a watery grave. According to Maroon oral tradition, her magic was so formidable that she was able to catch cannonballs between her buttocks and fart them back with deadly effect. Such stories may distort Nanny's true abilities, but like most legendary figures, her reputation was built around a solid kernel of truth.[4]

Nanny's role as a community leader is well established. In a 1938 study of Maroon history that relied heavily on the oral testimony of the Accompong Maroons, the story recounted that 'six members of an Ashanti family, consisting of five brothers, Cudjoe, Accompong, Johnny, Cuffee and Quaco, and one sister, Nanny, made their escape from slavery and assumed leadership of the Maroons'.[5] There are several references to Nanny in the records of contemporary European observers and militiamen. When captured by a British foraging party in 1735, an Igbo slave named Cupid revealed that 'a gang of about forty rebellious men, with a far greater number of women and children . . . were intending to make their way across to Cuffee's Town on the Leeward side of the island'. Among the members of the party he named were Nanny and her husband, whom he described as 'a greater man than Adou [the headman, who] never went into battles'.[6] Presumably, Nanny's importance was reflected in her husband's elevated status, which exempted him from battle.

Nanny's journey into slavery is undocumented, but it is thought that she and her brothers were captured from an Asante village and sold to a plantation in St Thomas before escaping into the Blue Mountains. Her leadership of the Windward Maroons in what was later called Nanny Town earned her a fearsome reputation. Summoned into battle by the blowing of an *abeng*, an animal horn, her warriors used guerrilla tactics to foil numerous British attacks on their mountain stronghold. She also organised successful raids on local plantations, seizing food and weapons and freeing many hundreds of slaves. This ten-year war of resistance only ended when the British, despairing of ever subduing them, offered the Maroons a peace treaty in exchange for land and guaranteed autonomy.

Captain Philip Thicknesse, who wrote a detailed account of his experience of leading a raid against the Blue Mountain Maroons, was probably referring to Nanny when he described the ferocious-looking obeah woman who was part of the Windward Maroon delegation at the signing of this peace treaty in 1739. Thicknesse, who lived with the Maroons for a period of time when they took him hostage, recalls that she wore 'a girdle round her waste [sic] . . . with nine or ten different knives hanging in sheaths to it, many of which . . . no doubt have been plunged into human flesh and blood'.[7]

Despite rumours of her death, Nanny is believed to have lived to enjoy the fruits of her struggles. According to the

Jamaican commissioner's records, permission was granted 'for Negro Nanny and the people residing with her [to live] on 500 acres of land in the Parish of Portland'.[8] Edward Long's census of the Maroon population, published in 1749, confirmed that once the peace treaty was concluded, Nanny and her followers chose not to settle with the main Windward party but broke away to found New Nanny Town. The Portland Maroons refer to it as 'Women's Town' because it was known as a haven for women, children and non-combatant men. The site of Nanny's grave is still revered by them, its location marked to this day by an area of untilled earth on which no one is permitted to build or grow provisions.[9]

Nanny's importance as a fighter and leader raises some intriguing questions about the status of Maroon women. They are typically described as slaves or drudges, the hapless victims of plunder by marauding males whose very survival depended on seizing women from local plantations. As always, this view was based on accounts by European men who tended to believe their own hype. Their preconceived notions of Africans and the 'dark continent' tainted whatever they saw. Characterising African women as brutalised and debauched amounted to an act of self-exoneration, for it allowed them to present their own much greater crime against Africans as a necessary 'civilising' intervention.[10]

The efforts of European militias to re-enslave or exterminate the Maroons relied heavily on such crass justifications. Their provocative presence in the surrounding hills and forests served as a permanent reminder to plantation inmates that slavery was not, after all, the best of all possible worlds. While some Maroon women were undoubtedly seized against their will, the prevailing image of them as unwilling victims of savage desperados does not even begin to tell the full story. Maroon women, particularly new arrivals from Africa, knew only too well what it meant to be kidnapped. Having survived the experience once, possibly twice, many of them would have made a conscious choice to stay, preferring the perils of life as a Maroon to the prospect of spending the rest of their lives as slaves. Thicknesse hinted at this possibility when he recalled seeing Maroon women who 'in their savage resentment . . . wore rows of teeth of white men as ornaments'.[11]

A detailed field study conducted at the turn of the nineteenth century refers to Maroons of both sexes and all ages, who 'in their person and carriage . . . were erect and lofty, indicating a consciousness of superiority'. Maroon women were crucial to the Maroons' economic, military and demographic survival, despite (or perhaps because of) the fact that they were in a minority. Described as precious and willing members of these outlawed settlements, they were 'employed chiefly in the cultivation of their grounds; but this they did not account as an imposition on them by the men'.[12]

Far from being an oppressed and exploited minority, the study described an equal division of labour, with the women employed in tillage and the burning of trees, while the men divided their time between hunting, the building and repair of houses, the care of cattle and horses and the pursuit of trade. Marriage was 'by the consent of the women alone',[13] and in times of siege, those who did not play an active part in fighting or transporting provisions were treated as valuable possessions and carefully concealed.[14]

Outnumbered as they were, it seems that women, too, helped to re-erect Africa in the mountains of Jamaica, as well as in Brazil, Surinam and the many other colonies where Maroons maintained a presence. In fact, if the attitude of their sisters on the plantations is anything to go by, women were probably central to the Maroons' stubborn refusal to accept a way of life that was anything other than self-determined.

A more recent account of Maroon life and values in Crawford Town, Jamaica, provides a telling hint of what African self-determination might have looked like today if Europeans hadn't intervened. Describing their most outstanding characteristic as 'confidence', the Maroon descendant interviewed describes the current generation of young Maroons as

> intensely proud of their heritage but [they] never boast about it. They are taught never to disgrace themselves and are brought up by a rigid set of values that is replicated in every maroon community. Maroon parents know that it's 'not you alone that grow your pickney', so children are controlled not just by parents but by the community's values. Those controls still exist and explain the low level of crime in maroon communities, where murders are virtually unknown.[15]

These values, instilled in young people from an early age, suggest a community coherence that is both robust and enduring. His description echoes much earlier accounts by Europeans in Africa. For example, Paul Erdmann Isert, who was appointed chief surgeon to the Danish forts and trading posts along the Guinea coast in 1783, studied in detail the coastal inhabitants of what is now present-day Ghana. In his letters home, he observed that 'crime is committed only rarely . . . (and) murder hardly ever occurs here' – a far cry from today's inner-city stereotype, with its prevalence of knife and gun crime.

Isert spent close to six years living among the 'Akras'. He took part in their wars and journeyed inland, so his experience was far from idealised. The people he encountered were polygamous, believed in obeah, and had 'no concept of hell'. Yet he described a society in which adultery was 'punished more frequently than robbery' if only because, prior to the arrival of 'Christians who instruct the Blacks in sin', robbery was 'hardly ever known to occur'. With maize, fruit, game and fish in abundance, 'the Blacks' needs were few, and they had a surplus of the things they needed, so they felt no necessity to steal'. Instead, they preferred to dance and play musical instruments and had 'a taste for amusement' and 'games . . . as numerous as they are inventive, and they spend most of their time in such enjoyment'.[16]

Memories of this stolen existence would have sustained and inspired the Maroons as they set about rebuilding their lives in the New World. The women who helped to establish these Afrocentric enclaves were, like women everywhere, the main repository of the diverse cultures that sustained them, so their role would have been crucial. This is true not only of Maroon women, with their obvious advantage of an independent existence beyond the planters' control, but also of their enslaved sisters down on the plantations, who could often only emulate such efforts.

Motherhood, for all its attendant suffering, was instrumental in this endeavour. Despite planters' concerted efforts to destroy all identification with the motherland, they were unable to stamp out the early bonds between enslaved mothers and their natural or surrogate children. Some women were reluctant or unable to conceive, others rejected the role completely for reasons we've already explored. But those who did bear children and managed to hold on to them clearly did everything in their power to honour their remembered maternal role.

According to Isert, it was a role in which 'the Blacks show an extraordinary tenderness towards their children . . . [and] almost never strike them'. Moreover, 'every single house or family is obliged to take care of its own members'.[17] These relationships must have been sorely tested under slavery, and brutalisation is known to breed its own brutality, but as planter William Beckford noted in his memoirs, most enslaved women 'exercise(d) a kind of sovereignty over their children which never cease(d) during life . . . the affections between mothers and even spurious offspring [being] very powerful as well as permanent'.[18]

Enforced separations and arbitrary sales meant that orphans and 'spurious offspring' were a fact of life on most West Indian plantations. By embracing and nurturing children who were not their own, women gained both respect in their communities and influence across their extended and surrogate families. These precarious, often short-lived attachments were no less sincere. Monk Lewis spoke of a woman with two sick children, one of whom she'd adopted when its own mother died in childbirth: 'There she sits', he wrote, 'throwing her eyes from one to the other with such increasing solitude, that no one would discover which was her own child and which was the orphan.'[19] He had good cause for concern, for the agony of losing a child was enough to tip some women over the edge. Planters often warned against separating mothers from their children, for it was said to drive them to '(sink) into utter despondency or put period to their lives'.[20]

Numerous eyewitnesses have spoken of the strong kinship ties that sustained enslaved communities, and most had no reason to romanticise what they observed. William Beckford described the slaves he encountered in Jamaica as 'in general attached to their families . . . and . . . much disposed to pay age respect and veneration'.[21] Stedman, admittedly a more sympathetic witness, maintained that 'no people can have more esteem or have a greater friendship for one another than the negro slaves . . . (who) appear to have an unbounded joy in each other's company'.[22] References to friends and family members who risked life and limb to harbour runaways can be found in archives across the West Indies.

When birth mothers were absent, as was often the case, the enduring African practice of caring for other women's children allowed older women to fill their shoes. While mothers toiled in the fields and mill-houses, their offspring would be placed under the supervision of an elderly woman, whose role was to show them the ropes and supervise their chores. It was under her influence that young children's sense of self and view of the world took shape. Older motherless slaves and those with no family ties would typically be 'adopted', ensuring that they too had access to the customs and folklore that were handed down from one generation to the next.

Thanks to these bonds, Akan, Igbo and other African cultural continuities survived and thrived across the

Caribbean. Motherhood, in all its complex forms, under-pinned socio-economic activities and kinship ties on every plantation, facilitating the transfer of knowledge and skills. Mary Seacole's relationship with her mother is a perfect example. Mary, who learnt her craft as a child and went on to nurse the casualties of the Crimean War, was inspired by her Jamaican mother's skills as a 'doctoress' and tradi-tional healer. Her mother, a free black woman, ran a lodging house in Kingston, and was highly esteemed for her medical services. As her mother's assistant from the age of twelve, Mary gained an early interest in medicine and caring for the sick. The medical prowess she learnt at her mother's elbow would determine the course of her life. According to Mary, she also had her mother to thank for her indomitable independent spirit and her unwavering confidence in her own skills power.[23]

Among the resources that African-born women carried with them was a strong sense of their own self-worth, instilled in them from their earliest experience of socialisa-tion. Their clearly defined sexual, domestic, childbearing and economic roles gave them prestige and authority within their original communities, making it possible for both enslaved and elite women to hold high office in most areas of public life as rulers, priestesses, soldiers or govern-ment officials.

It's important to remember that this wasn't true of all the African cultures that helped shape enslaved societies. Nor should this image of female self-worth detract from the less palatable truth that West Africa was essentially a patriarchal domain that favoured and elevated men. As

Isert observed, it was common for men to have several wives, a practice that was exported wholesale onto the plantation. Women could also be beaten, excommunicated or executed, particularly when accused of witchcraft. As in Europe, they were often victims of their community's ignorance and superstition. But it was also a cultural environment in which associations between the sexes were carefully defined and regulated.

In most West African societies, it was biological differ-ence rather than a sense of inferiority that defined women's role. The traditional rituals marking young girls' initiation into womanhood gave them a clear sense of their biologi-cal, social and spiritual roles. Having learnt about their central importance in relation to sex, marriage, childbirth, motherhood, death and the widespread system of matriar-chal inheritance, they would have come away with an understanding that, as women, they were the principal guardians and perpetuators of the life cycle. Even young girls transported from Africa would have acquired a sense of these functions and responsibilities by the time they entered the plantation.[24]

Jamaican historian Edward Kamau Braithwaite has argued that the this diverse and constantly adapting African culture was able to resist its own destruction because it was 'carried within the individual (or) commu-nity, not (as in Europe) . . . externalised in buildings, monuments, books, "the artefacts of civilisation" . . . Dance was African architecture . . . history was not printed but recited'. In practice, this meant that each transported African carried within them 'the potential of reconstruc-tion . . . the ability to use, starting with nothing more than his [sic] nakedness and breath, a whole range of remarkably complex resources'.[25]

In many of the cultures represented on West Indian plantations, women were at the very heart of the web of relationships that regulated the community's existence. They also took strength and comfort from a spiritual life that was grounded in the veneration of their ancestors and drew energy from the power of collective worship. European chroniclers, with their blinkered view of Africa and plantation life, failed to recognise the many subtle ways this empowered and elevated women of African descent when they chose to embrace it. Women's experience of enslavement may have distorted their perceptions of self and society, and as more and more people were born unfree, these had to be constantly redefined. Yet both African-born and Creole women were able to preserve and pass on a set of values and beliefs, rituals and practices that enabled each new generation to resist and surmount the grim realities they encountered.

The enslaved African woman's status, as these pages bear witness, meant that she was the bearer of many of her race's heaviest burdens. But it also ensured that she remained, in Lucille Mair's words, the carrier of its roots.[26] The mothers who admonished or soothed their children with Anancy stories, and the grandmothers who passed on memories of their African past, are owed a huge debt of gratitude. They played a vital role as they moulded and reshaped the cultural traditions that would sustain their people through centuries of tyranny, so that we, their distant kin and scattered descendants, would know our own worth. Thanks to their courage and their refusal to be cowed, black and brown women have inherited a wealth of inner resources and a heritage to proud of.

We have much to be grateful for.

Afterword

Researching and writing this book may have assuaged my nine-year-old hunger for a history that included women like me, but this story is far from over. Enslavement, kidnapping and trafficking of people continue to plague our world on a mind-numbing scale, and women of African descent continue to be victims of the most appalling gendered barbarity. Fighting these ongoing injustices is by far the best way to honour the vow engraved on that plaque in Elmina.

The parallels with the past are all too stark. The horrors of the middle passage are echoed in stories of African women and girls staggering across the Sahara desert, suffering rape and abuse in their desperation to escape war and poverty. As recently as November 2017, the European Network of Migrant Women released the following statement about the 'femicide' of young West African females:

Over 26 West African females, suspected to be from Nigeria and aged 14–18, have been found dead in the Mediterranean Sea in the recent days. The death of migrants at sea, from being a 'tragedy' once, has now become a 'norm' in Europe. In the case of Sub Saharan females whose lives have been lost en route to Europe, it is an outcome of the border management aggressively pursued by the European institutions. It is also an outcome of systemic male violence perpetrated against women at every stage of their journeys, outside and within Europe.[1]

Reports like this should inspire the same degree of outrage today as anything we've encountered in these pages.

The causes of human trafficking in Africa are complex, but its consequences are global. Of the estimated 800,000 people trafficked across international borders each year, a disproportionate number originate in Africa. In 2016, around 80 per cent of the 11,000 migrant women who arrived in Italy had come from Nigeria. Their prospects of avoiding prostitution or being trafficked across borders for sex were slim. Meanwhile, across the African continent, female genitals are mutilated, mothers and grandmothers are gang raped by marauding soldiers, and girls as young as eight years old are sold as 'brides'.[2]

Senseless wars continue to cause misery and displacement for millions, and the parameters haven't really changed. According to the Campaign Against Arms Trade, since January 2016, the value of approved UK military exports to countries in sub-Saharan Africa has amounted to well over £200 million. European guns and weaponry bolster the most corrupt, self-serving regimes, ensuring that even now, centuries after they first appeared on her shores, Africa's human and mineral resources are still there for the taking. It was private companies that spearheaded the plunder of Africa all those years ago, and they continue to do so to this day. The degree of profiteering from African labour and resources has hardly changed, and the beneficiaries haven't changed much, either. The corruption of wealthy African leaders prepared to sell their country's resources to all comers and pocket the proceeds should create the same level of fury as those early African chiefs who exchanged their people for guns.

Caribbean countries face similar challenges. The failure of their erstwhile colonisers to invest in any meaningful economic development post-slavery has meant that poverty remains a scourge. Far too many descendants of the enslaved continue to live in abject conditions. The levels of disease, hunger, and illiteracy are an indictment of those who profit from such misery and this should inspire loud demands for transparency, accountability and change. If anything is to be learnt from this shared history of ours, it is that our capacity to challenge its legacies remains largely untapped.

Whether reparations can address these issues is an ongoing debate. Unless the money is targeted at those who have suffered most as a direct result of slavery and used to finance better schooling, for example, or improved housing, sanitation and healthcare, it could well disappear into the coffers of governments and institutions that do little to challenge slavery's legacies. How much is owed is unquantifiable, and given what we know about the extent of African involvement, there is also the awkward question of who is liable. By buying into a Eurocentric version of slavery that presents Africans solely as victims, do we risk denying them their agency?

Another problem with financial reparations is that money cannot begin to address the deeply ingrained racist attitudes that are now so embedded in our society. The so-called 'Windrush' scandal, as well as the hostile environment that led to the expulsion of countless British Caribbean citizens who contributed to Britain's post-war development, is a stark reminder that black people's labour remains exploited and undervalued to this day. Decades of toil for the mother country were ignored as individuals were denied their right to British citizenship and sent back to the countries from which they came. For the victims of this outrage, men and women alike, the parallels must have been all too stark. Having slaved all their lives, they remained as expendable as their ancestors. If anything, the racism that underpinned these expulsions is on the rise.

The most enduring lessons from this history of female resilience have yet to be learnt – lessons about survival, community and human dignity that can motivate and inspire us. Whether an interested onlooker, a direct descendant or, as in my own case, an admiring distant relative, their example is a powerful call to action. The headstrong women whose acts of resistance litter these pages are owed a huge debt of gratitude. The best way to honour them is to emulate their example until slavery's dark stain, in all its manifestations, is finally and permanently removed.

Notes

Acknowledgements
1. A Fante expression of gratitude, in response to something done or given.

Epigraphs
1. L. M. Mair, *The Rebel Woman in the British West Indies During Slavery* (Kingston: Institute of Jamaica, 1975).
2. Harriet Jacobs, 'Incidents in the Life of a Slave Girl' in *I was Born a Slave, Volume 2* (Edinburgh: Payback Press, 1999).
3. Matthew 'Monk' Lewis, *Journal of a West India Proprietor, Kept During a Residence in the Island of Jamaica* (London: Murray, 1824), 389.

Introduction
1. Barbara Bush, 'Defiance or Submission? The Role of Black Women in Slave Resistance in the British Caribbean',

Immigrants & Minorities 1: 1, 1982, 16.

2. George Jackson's book, *Soledad Brother: The Prison Letters of George Jackson* (New York: Penguin, 1973), combines his autobiography with a radical manifesto for black liberation. His memory is closely associated with Angela Davis, who was accused of supplying the weapons used in a foiled attempt to free Jackson and the two other Soledad Brothers from jail in 1970. She became a fugitive but was later tried, imprisoned and acquitted.

3. For example, see Michael Jordan, *The Great Abolition Sham* (Stroud: Sutton, 2005), who argues that it was thanks to manoeuvring by Wilberforce's sons that Clarkson, the real force behind the abolition movement, received so little credit.

4. See Eric Williams, *Capitalism and Slavery* (Chapel Hill: University of North Carolina Press, 1944); C. L. R. James, *The Black Jacobins: Toussaint L'Ouverture and The San Domingo Revolution* (London: Secker & Warburg, 1938); Walter Rodney *How Europe Underdeveloped Africa* (London: Bogle-L'Ouverture, 1972); Herbert Gutman *The Black Family in Slavery and Freedom* (New York: Vintage, 1976); and Eugene Genovese, *From Rebellion to Revolution: Afro-American Slave Revolts in the Making of the New World* (Baton Rouge: Louisiana State University Press, 1979).

5. Quote from the song *Columbus*, written by Winston Rodney (Burning Spear, 'Hail H. I. M.', 1980).

6. Eric Williams's theory, linking the demise of slavery with changes in Britain's imperial economy and the rise of 'laissez -faire' capitalism has since been challenged – see Seymour Drescher, 'The Decline Thesis of British Slavery since Econocide', *Slavery & Abolition*, 7: 1, 1986, 3–23.

7. Mary Prince was brought to England from Antigua by her

fourth master, James Woods. After the Somerset case ruled that it was no longer legal to transport enslaved people from England, she left his household and began working for Thomas Pringle, founder of the Anti-Slavery Society, who arranged for her story to be transcribed. The publication of her autobiography in 1831 caused much controversy, and she was twice called upon to defend it against accusations of libel. However, it was widely read and did much to bolster the abolitionists' cause.

Chapter 1

1. Royal African Company records, T/70/51, quoted in Nigel Tattersfield, *The Forgotten Trade* (London: Pimlico, 1991), 90.

2. For more on Ana Nzinga, see Linda M. Heywood, *Njinga of Angola* (Cambridge: Harvard University Press, 2017).

3. For more on Amina, see Bonnie G. Smith, *The Oxford Encyclopedia of Women in World History* (Oxford: Oxford University Press, 2008), 101.

4. For more on Beatriz, see John K. Thornton, *The Kongolese Saint Anthony: Dona Beatriz Kimpa Vita and the Antonian Movement, 1684–1706* (Cambridge: Cambridge University Press, 1998).

5. Queen mother Nana Yaa Asantewaa of West Africa's Ashanti Empire, Black History Heroes, retrieved 20 February 2017, quoted in Wikipedia. For more about Yaa Asantewaa, see A. Adu Boahen, Yaa Asantewaa and the Ashanti-British War of 1900–1 (New York: James Currey, 2003).

6. Pip Jones, *Satan's Kingdom: Bristol and the Transatlantic Slave Trade* (Bristol: Past & Present Press, 2007), 54–7.

7. Agaja's precise motives remain hotly disputed; there are some

historians who interpret his motives very differently, claiming that he was simply interested in consolidating his own power and influence. For more on this debate see the Wikipedia entry for Agaja.

8. See Edna G. Bay, *Wives of the Leopard, Gender, Politics and Culture in the Kingdom of Dahomey* (Charlottesville: University of Virginia Press, 1998), 11.

9. Tattersfield, *The Forgotten Trade*, 20.

10. A Danish surgeon who witnessed the fighting during the Sagbadre war of 1784 observed that 'a great number of our men were injured when their guns exploded, with the result that either the entire left hand, or part of it, was lost. For this misfortune we are indebted to a new kind of musket which has been sent to us in recent years. See Paul Erdmann Isert, *Letters on West Africa and the Slave Trade* (Oxford: Sub-Saharan Publishers, 2007), 15.

11. For more on the early period of the Atlantic slave trade and the involvement of the Royal African Company, see Eric Williams's account in 'Capitalism and Slavery' in *From Columbus to Castro: The History of the Caribbean 1492–1969* (London: Oxford University Press, 1970), 126–35.

12. Report of the Yearly Committee of England's Society of Friends, 1808.

13. Francis Moore, *Travels into the Inland Parts of Africa* (London: Edward Cave, 1738).

14. Instructions from the Royal African Company to the King of Whydah, quoted in David W. Galenson, *Traders, Planters and Slaves: Market Behaviour in Early English America* (Cambridge: Cambridge University Press, 1986), 112–13.

15. Verney Lovett Cameron, *Across Africa* (New York: Harper and Brothers, 1877), 357.

16. Although the slave trade was officially abolished by Britain in 1807, some other European countries – notably Spain and Portugal – continued to transport Africans to the Americas for another eighty years, primarily to Cuba and Brazil. As coastal communities became depleted, Portuguese traders, who tended to source their slaves from Angola and the Congo, were increasingly dependent on captives brought from the interior. Arab slavers were also active in the region, meaning that sights such as this were far from rare.

17. Mungo Park, *Travels in the Interior of Africa* (Edinburgh: A & C Black, 1858), 273–86.

18. Thomas Clarkson, *The Substance of the Evidence of Sundry Persons on the Slave-Trade, Collected in the Course of a Tour made in the Autumn of 1788* (London: James Phillips, 1789).

19. Ibid.

20. Ibid.

21. David Robinson, *Muslim Societies in African History* (Cambridge: Cambridge University Press, 2004), 61–3.

22. See Richard Rathbone, 'Some Thoughts on Resistance to Enslavement' in G. Heuman (ed.) *Out of the House of Bondage: Runaways, Resistance and Marronage in Africa and the New World* (London: Routledge, 1986).

23. For more on the treatment of local women and their children by European men, see William St Clair, *The Grand Slave Emporium* (London: Profile Books, 2006), 149–70.

24. John Thornton, *Africa and the Africans in the Making of the Atlantic World* (New York: Cambridge University Press, 1992), 66.

25. Thomas Phillips, 'A Voyage Made in the "Hannibal"' of London, 1693–94', in George Francis Dow, *Slave Ships and Slaving* (New York: Dover Publications, 2002), 55.

26. Isert, *Letters on West Africa and the Slave Trade*, 208–9.

27. For more on relationships between European men and local women, see St Clair, *The Grand Slave Emporium*, 149–60.

28. Hugh Thomas, *The Slave Trade* (New York: Simon & Schuster, 1997), 340–2.

29. For more on Betsy Heard, see the references included in her Wikipedia entry under Betsy Heard.

30. For more on the difficulties of procuring slaves, see Jones, *Satan's Kingdom*, 95.

31. John Bardot, quoted in E. Donnan, *Documents Illustrative of the History of the Slave Trade to America, Volume 1* (Washington: Carnegie Institution of Washington, 1930–1935), 293.

32. Thomas Phillips, 'A Voyage Made in the "Hannibal"' of London, 1693–94', 61.

33. See Alexander Falconbridge's account in Thomas Howard (ed.) *Black Voyage – Eyewitness Accounts of the Atlantic Slave Trade* (Boston: Little, Brown, 1971).

34. See Chapter 1 of Olaudah Equiano, *The Interesting Narrative of Olaudah Equiano* (New York: Penguin Classics, 2003).

Chapter 2

1. Ibid.

2. David Richardson, 'Shipboard Revolts, African Authority and the Atlantic Slave Trade', *William & Mary Quarterly*, 58, 2001, 69–92.

3. Hugh Thomas, *The Slave Trade*, 423.

4. William Bosman, *A New and Accurate Description of the Coast of Guinea* (London, 1705), 365.

5. G. Williams, *History of the Liverpool Privateers and Letters of Marque with an Account of the Liverpool Slave Trade* (1897)

quoted in Hilary Beckles, *Natural Rebels, A Social History of Enslaved Black Women in Barbados* (New Brunswick, NJ: Rutgers University Press, 1989), 155.

6. Elizabeth Donnan, *Documents Illustrative of the History of the Slave Trade to America, Volume 3* (Washington: Carnegie Institution of Washington, 1930–1935), 118–21.

7. Ibid.

8. Ibid.

9. William Snelgrave, *A New Account of Some Parts of Guinea and the Slave Trade* (London, 1734).

10. *Calibar Historical Journal*, 1, 1, quoted in Beckles, 155.

11. Falconbridge in Howard (ed.) *Black Voyage*.

12. James Walvin, *The Zong* (New Haven: Yale University Press, 2011), 97.

13. Thomas, *The Slave Trade*, 426.

14. For a comparative overview of the length of the middle passage by region, see D. Eltis, S. Behrendt, D. Richardson and H. Klein, *The Atlantic Slave Trade: A Database* on CD-Rom (Cambridge: Cambridge University Press, 1999).

15. For more on the numbers debate, see Paul E. Lovejoy, *Transformations in Slavery* (Cambridge: Cambridge University Press, 2000), who estimates that between 1650 and 1900, the total number of slaves exported to the Americas was 10,240,200; and Hugh Thomas, *The Slave Trade*, who estimates that the total number of imported slaves between 1450 and 1900 was 11,328.000. Of these, two million (17.7 per cent) were sold to planters in the British West Indies.

16. Dow, *Slave Ships and Slaving*, 174.

17. Donnan, *Documents Illustrative of the History of the Slave Trade to America, Volume 1*, 498.

18. Ottobah Cugoano, *Thoughts and Sentiments on the Evil and Wicked Traffic of the Slavery and Commerce of the Human Species, Humbly Submitted to the Inhabitants of Great Britain* (London 1787), 10.

19. John Newton, *Thoughts Upon the African Slave Trade* (London: J. Row, 1788).

20. Barbara Bush, *Slave Women in Caribbean Society, 1650–1832* (Bloomington: Indiana University Press, 1990), 57.

21. Black crew members, some of whom were former slaves, were particularly suspect. Their role as interpreters and their ability to communicate or sympathise with the captives made them capable of switching sides. As late as 1812, just off the coast of Benguela, a group of enslaved sailors are known to have joined a below-decks revolt on board the Portuguese ship *Feliz Eugenia*, escaping in small boats along with many of the children. See Mariana P. Candido's article, 'Different Slave Journeys: Enslaved African Seamen on Board Portuguese Ships c. 1760–1820s', *Slavery & Abolition*, 31, 3, 2010, 395–409.

22. Reverend John Riland, *Memoirs of a West Indian Planter* (London, 1837).

23. Donnan, *Documents Illustrative of the History of the History of the Slave Trade, Volume 2*, 403.

24. Jones, *Satan's Kingdom*, 38.

25. Donnan, *Documents Illustrative of the History of the History of the Slave Trade, Volume 2*, 321.

26. Sir Hans Sloane, *A Voyage to the Islands of Madeira, Barbados, Nieves, St Christopher and Jamaica* (London, 1707) – quoted in Bush, *Slave Women in Caribbean Society* (London: James Currey, 1990), 55.

27. Jaques Savary, *The Perfect Merchant or General Instruction*

regarding the mercantile trade of France and foreign countries, 1675.

28. R. Sheridan, *Doctors and Slaves: A Medical and Demographic History of Slavery in the West Indies, 1680–1834* (Cambridge: Cambridge University Press, 1985), 122–3, based on evidence taken from Matthew Morley's *A Guinea Surgeon's Journals* (1788–1789).

29. Olaudah Equiano, *The Interesting Narrative of Olaudah Equiano.*

30. Thomas, *The Slave Trade*, 198–201.

31. See Eric Williams, *Capitalism and Slavery* (Chapel Hill: University of North Carolina Press, 1944), 52.

32. J. F. Nicholls and J. Taylor, *Bristol Past & Present* (Bristol: J.W. Arrowsmith, 1881).

33. Folarin Shyllon, *Black People in England* (London: Oxford University Press, 1977), 6–7.

34. See Jones, *Satan's Kingdom*, 44–8.

35. Dalby Thomas – quoted in Eric Williams *Capitalism and Slavery* (Chapel Hill: University of North Carolina Press, 1944). For more on Liverpool's involvement in the triangular trade, see Anthony Tibbles' paper, *Liverpool and the Slave Trade* (London: Gresham College, 2007).

36. Hannah Moore, 'Slavery', see poetryfoundation.org.

37. For more information about the women who campaigned for the abolition of the slave trade, see brycchancarey.com.

38. *Bristol Gazette*, 12 June 1788.

39. Olaudah Equiano, (New York: Penguin Classics, 2003).

Chapter 3

1. Nanny's remains are believed to be buried at 'Bump Grave' in Moore Town.

2. Michael Craton, *Testing the Chains* (Ithaca: Cornell University Press, 1982), 336–7.

3. Ibid., 91–2.

4. The debate about the true number of women transported from Africa is ongoing. See David Eltis and Stanley L. Engerman, 'Was the Slave Trade Dominated by Men?' *Journal of Interdisciplinary History*, 23, 2, 1992, 237–57.

5. For more on the role of the Akan in slave rebellions, see Monica Schuler, 'Akan Slave Rebellions in the British Caribbean' in *Caribbean Slave Society and Economy*, eds. H. Beckles & V. Shepherd (London: James Currey, 1991), 373–86.

6. The Centre for the Study of the Legacies of British Slave Ownership has compiled a comprehensive database of Britons who received compensation when slavery was abolished – see ucl.ac.uk.

7. See Richard Sheridan, 'Simon Taylor, Sugar Tycoon on Jamaica 1740–1813', *Agricultural History*, XLV, 1971, 287, in which he claims that absentee landlords owned 30 per cent of Jamaica's sugar estates in 1775, rising to 84 per cent in just over half a century.

8. Jamaica also produced significant quantities of coffee, cotton, ginger, pimento, dyewoods and hardwood. See Verene A. Shepherd, 'Trade and Exchange in Jamaica in the Period of Slavery' in *Caribbean Slave Society and Economy*, eds. H. Beckles & V. Shepherd (London: James Currey, 1991).

9. See Michael Craton's 'Death, Disease and Medicine on the Jamaican Slave Plantations: The Example of Worthy Park 1767–1838' in Beckles and Shepherd, *Caribbean Slave Society and Economy*.

10. Richard S. Dunn, A Tale of Two Plantations: Slave Life at

Mesopotamia in Jamaica & Mount Airy in Virginia 1799–1828, *William & Mary Quarterly*, 24, 1977, 54.

11. See Beckles, 30–32, 91.

12. C. O. 101/65 President Paterson to Earl Bathurst Grenada, 23 November 1825, No 80, f.116 – quoted in Nicole Phillip, *Producers, Reproducers and Rebels: Grenadian Slave Women 1783–1833*, paper presented at Grenada Country Conference, January 2002, open.uwi.edu.

13. For more on the situation of women field workers in the French Antilles, see Bernard Moitt's 'Women, Work and Resistance in the French Caribbean during Slavery, 1700–1848', in *Engendering History: Caribbean Women in Perspective* eds. Verene Shepherd, Bridget Brereton and Barbara Bailey (London: James Currey, 1995), 158–63.

14. For a more detailed exploration of these findings, see R. Sheridan, *Sugar & Slavery: An Economic History of the British West Indies, 1623–1775* (Baltimore: Johns Hopkins University Press, 1974), 257–8.

15. R. S. Dunn, 'A Tale of Two Plantations', 45, claims, for example, that '[a]t Mesopotamia, as was generally the case on West Indian sugar estates, females proved tougher than the males and better able to survive the trauma of slavery'.

16. William Dickson, *Letters on Slavery*, 1789 (Negro University Press [reprint], 1970).

17. Justin Girod-Chantrans, *Voyage d'un Suisse dans differentes colonies d'Amerique*, 1785 reprint (Paris: Tallandier, 1980), 131 – quoted in Moitt's 'Women, Work and Resistance in the French Caribbean during Slavery, 1700–1848', 158.

18. See Sheridan *Doctors and Slaves*, 150.

19. Dickson, *Letters on Slavery*.

20. For more on the status of white women in the Caribbean,

see Hilary Beckles' 'Sex and Gender in the Historiography of Caribbean Slavery' in *Engendering History*, 125–40, in which he suggests that '*the white woman was . . . considered unfit for manual labour on account of her endemic fragility; unsuited to physical exertion in the tropic as a consequence of her possession of a faint heart and a delicate skin*'. He points out that while this was true of propertied white women and those deemed respectable, working-class women who came as indentured labourers were viewed very differently and variously described as 'loose wenches', 'whores', 'sluts', and white niggers'.

21. Janet Shaw, *Journal of a Lady of Quality: Being the Narrative of a Journey from Scotland to the West Indies, North Carolina & Portugal in the years 1774 to 1776*, eds. E. W. and C. M. Andrews (New Haven: Yale University Press, 1939) – as quoted in 'Text, Testimony & Gender: An Examination of Some Texts by Women on the English Speaking Caribbean from the 1770s to the 1920s' by Bridget Brereton in *Engendering History*, 75.

22. Galenson, *Traders, Planters and Slaves*, 63.

23. Bush, *Defiance or Submission*, 22.

24. See Phillip, *Producers, Reproducers and Rebels*.

25. C. O. 110/107 – List of Negroes in the Upper Pearls estate, taken January 1802, quoted in Nicole Phillip, *Producers, Reproducers and Rebels*.

26. For more on this argument, see Bush, 'Towards Emancipation: Slave Women & Resistance to Coercive Labour Regimes in the British West Indian Colonies (1770–1838)' in D. Richardson (ed.) *Abolition and its Aftermath: The Historical Context 1790–1916* (London: Frank Cass, 1985).

27. See *The History of Mary Prince, A West Indian Slave, Related by Herself* (Makati: Pandora, 1987), 23. Mary was born in Bermuda around 1788, and worked in Bermuda, the Turks Islands and Antigua before being brought to England by her owners in 1828. Originally published in 1831, hers is the only surviving account of slavery by a Caribbean woman.

28. Jean-Baptiste (Père) Labat, *Nouveau Voyage Aux Isles de l'Amerique* (6 volumes), Paris 1722, as quoted in Moitt's 'Women, Work and Resistance in the French Caribbean during Slavery, 1700–1848', 165.

29. Quoted in Sheridan, *Doctors and Slaves*, 227.

30. Sheridan (ibid., 150) cites the evidence of Jamaican attorney William Taylor, who testified to the Select Committee on the Extinction of Slavery that cane-hole digging had a particularly detrimental effect on the female frame and was the chief cause of the continuing decrease in slaves.

31. Barbados Committee Report, 1789, quoted in Bush, 'Towards Emancipation', 130.

32. See Michael Craton, 'Death, Disease and Medicine on the Jamaican Slave Plantations: the Example of Worthy Park 1767–1838', *Social History*, 9, 1976, 237–55, in which Craton analyses the specific causes of death of 401 slaves.

33. Richard Sheridan, *Doctors and Slaves*, 169.

34. Food Allowance on Bayley's and Thickett's estates, included in the *Report for a Select Committee of the House of Assembly Appointed to Inquire into the Origins, Causes and Progress of the Late Insurrections, Barbados*, 1817, quoted in Beckles, 44.

35. Monk Lewis, *Journal of a Residence Among the Negroes in the West Indies*, 14 January 1816, 103–4.

36. Ibid., 13 January 1816, 96.

37. H. J. Bennett, 'The Problem of Slave Labor Supply at the

Codrington Plantations', *Journal of Negro History*, 36, 1951, 406–41.

38. Grenadian Public Record Office: 71437 – quoted in Nicole Phillip, *Producers, Reproducers and Rebels: Grenadian Slave Women 1783–1833*.

39. Sessional Papers, Vol. 82, 1791/92 – quoted in Women Slaves and Rebels in Grenada, Brigitte Kossek, publications. iai.spk-berlin.de.

40. In South Carolina, for example, the number of slaves on one plantation is said to have increased from eighty-six to 270 within just thirty-five years, with only twelve or fourteen purchases. (See *The Letters & Papers of Henry Laurens*, quoted in Hugh Thomas, *The Slave Trade*, 269).

Chapter 4

1. Letter from General Murray to the British Government, 24 August 1823 (*British Parliamentary Papers: Correspondence and Papers Relating to Slavery and the Abolitionist of the Slave Trade 1831–34*, Vol. 66).

2. Harry J. Bennett, *Bondsmen and Bishops: Slavery and Apprenticeship on the Codrington Plantations of Barbados* (Berkeley: University of California Press, 1958), 30–1.

3. Ian Duffield, *From Slave Colonies to Penal Colonies: The West Indian Convict Colonies Transportees to Australia*, quoted in Bush, *Slave Women in Caribbean Society*, 81.

4. Prince, *The History of Mary Prince, A West Indian Slave, Related by Herself*, 3.

5. John Stedman, *Narrative of a Five-Year Expedition against the Revolted Negroes of Surinam, 1772–1777* (London, 1796), 13–14.

6. Quoted in Bush, *Slave Women in Caribbean Society*, 42.

7. Prince, *The History of Mary Prince*, 6.

8. Thomas Cooper, *Facts Illustrative of the Condition of the Slaves in Jamaica* (London, 1824), 17–18.

9. Quoted in Bush, 'Defiance or Submission?', 20.

10. John Jeremie, Essays on Colonial Slavery 1831, quoted in Bush, 81.

11. Sheridan, *Doctors and Slaves*, 189.

12. James Williams, *Narrative of Events since the First of August 1834 by James Williams, an Apprenticed Labourer in Jamaica* (London, 1837), 9.

13. Sheridan, *Doctors and Slaves*, 242.

14. Reverent Henry Coor's evidence in British Sessional Papers, Commons, *Report of the Lords of Trade on the Slave Trade*, Vol. 26 (1789).

15. William Dickson, quoted in Beckles, 69.

16. Quoted in C. L. R. James, *The Black Jacobins: Toussaint L'Ouverture and the San Domingo Revolution* (New York: Vintage Books, 1963), 59.

17. Prince, *The History of Mary Prince*.

18. Craton, 'Death, Disease and Medicine on the Jamaican Slave Plantations, 44.

19. Ibid.

20. John Stedman, *Narrative of a Five-Year Expedition*, 279.

21. Elizabeth Fenwick's Letters (1814–1821) in A. F. Fenwick (ed.) *The Fate of the Fenwicks: Letters to Mary Hays, 1798–1828* (London: Methuen, 1927), 163–4.

22. Ibid., 169–70.

23. *Hampshire Telegraph*, 12 May 1823.

24. Sheridan, *Doctors and Slaves*, 243.

25. James Williams, *Narrative of Events*, 15.

26. Ibid., 10.

27. Janet Shaw, *Journal of a Lady of Quality: Being the Narrative of a Journey from Scotland to the West Indies, North Carolina and Portugal, in the years 1774 to 1776*, eds. E. W and C. M. Andrews (New Haven: Yale University Press, 1939), 112–13.

28. Elizabeth Fenwick's Letters, 169–70.

29. R. Hildreth, *The Ruin of Jamaica*, Anti-Slavery Tract No. 6, American Anti-Slavery Society, 1855.

30. Ibid.

31. For example, see discussion of O. Patterson's work by Fiona Greenland and George Steinmetz, 'Orlando Patterson, his work, and his legacy: a special issue in celebration of the republication of *Slavery and Social Death*', *Theory and Society*, 48, 2019, 785–97.

32. Edward Long, *The History of Jamaica* (London: T. Lowndes, 1774).

33. Mary Prince, *The History of Mary Prince*, 67.

34. *Thomas Thistlewood Journals (1748–1786)*, cited in Craton, 'Death, Disease and Medicine on the Jamaican Slave Plantations, 38–43.

35. Ibid.

36. Matthew 'Monk' Lewis, *Journal of a West India Proprietor*, 389.

Chapter 5

1. C. O. 101/65 President Paterson to Earl Bathurst, Grenada, 23 November 1825, No. 80, f.116. Quoted in Nicole Phillip, *Producers, Reproducers, and Rebels*.

2. Lewis, *Journal of a West India Proprietor*, 74

3. Ibid., 204.

4. Ibid.,139.

5. Ibid., 179.

6. Ibid., 183.

7. Stedman, *Narrative of a Five-Year Expedition*, 370.

8. Long, *The History of Jamaica*, 331.

9. Craton, 'Death, Disease and Medicine on the Jamaican Slave Plantations'.

10. Elizabeth Fenwick's Letters, 168.

11. Frances Lanaghan, *Antigua and the Antiguans, Volume 2* (London: Spottiswoode, 1967), 77–8.

12. Bridget Brereton, 'Text, Testimony and Gender: An Examination of some Texts by Women on the English-speaking Caribbean from the 1770s to the 1920s' in *Engendering History*, 68–9.

13. Examples cited in Bush, *Slave Women in Caribbean Society*, 58.

14. This reference and the other examples from Barbados given in the following paragraph, are quoted in H. M. Beckles, 166–8.

15. See Nicole Phillip, *Producers, Reproducers, and Rebels*, in which she points out that women accounted for 62 per cent, while men accounted for 38 per cent of 703 runaways.

16. For a more detailed account of the role women played in slave rebellions and uprisings, see Bush, 65–77.

17. Craton, 'Death, Disease and Medicine on the Jamaican Slave Plantations', 29.

18. This particular quote, attributed to Councillor Vallentine Morris, was included in an anonymous account entitled 'A Genuine Narrative of the Intended Conspiracy of the Negroes of Antigua' (Dublin, 1937) and is the subject of a paper by David B. Gasper entitled 'The Antigua Slave Conspiracy of 1736: A Case Study of the Origins of Collective Resistance', *William & Mary Quarterly*, 35, 1978, 308.

19. *Select Committee of the House of Assembly Appointed to Inquire*

into the Origins, Causes and Progress of the Late Insurrection (Barbados, 1818), 39, quoted in Beckles, 171–2.

20. 'Confession of Robert', ibid.

21. Obeah refers to a magical belief system practised in enslaved communities in the British West Indies.

22. Stedman, *Narrative of a Five-Year Expedition, Volume 11,* 304.

23. Craton, 'Death, Disease and Medicine on the Jamaican Slave Plantations', 132–85.

24. Craton, *Testing the Chains: Resistance to Slavery in the British West Indies* (Cornell University Press, 2009), 17.

25. Long, *The History of Jamaica Vol. II*, 445.

26. Bernard Senior, *A Retired Military Officer* (London, 1831), 180, 204–7, 212–16.

27. Bush, 'Defiance or Submission', 28.

28. William Smith, *A Natural History of Nevis, and the rest of the English Leeward Charibee Islands in America* (Cambridge, 1745), 230.

29. Assembly meeting minutes of 7 December 1753, C. O. 186/ 3. Both this and the previous reference appear in Natalie Zacek's article, 'Reading the rebels: currents of slave resistance in the eighteenth-century British West Indies', archives. history.ac.uk.

30. Lewis, *Journal of a West India Proprietor*, 397.

31. Lewis, *Journal of a West India Proprietor*, 149.

32. Quasheeba, like the name Quashee, is derived from common names found among the Akan peoples of modern Ghana. Quashee is probably a derivative of 'Kwesi', the name given to boy children born on a Sunday.

33. A more detailed description of Old Doll and her family is given by Beckles, 66–8.

34. Maria Nugent, *Lady Nugent's Diary* (London, 1839).

Chapter 6

1. B. W. Higman, *Slave Populations of the British Caribbean* (Baltimore: Johns Hopkins University Press, 1984), 74–5.
2. Kenneth Morgan, 'Slave Women and Reproduction in Jamaica, c. 1776–1834', *History* 91: 302, 2006.
3. Dickson, *Letters on Slavery*, 15–16.
4. Beckles, 100–1.
5. Dickson, *Letters on Slavery*, 155.
6. Governor Edward Trelawney, *An Essay Concerning Slavery* (1746), 35–6.
7. Sheridan, *Doctors and Slaves*, 45, 59.
8. Michael Craton and Walvin James, *A Jamaican Plantation: The History of Worthy Park 1670–1870* (Toronto: University of Toronto Press, 1970), quoted in Bush, 131.
9. André de Lacharière, *De l'affranchisement des esclaves dans les colonies Francaises* (Paris, 1836), 107, quoted in Moitt, 'Women, Work and Resistance', 161.
10. Gabriel Debien, *Les Esclaves aux Antilles Francaises, XVII-XVIII Siècle*, 129–30, quoted in Moitt, 'Women, Work and Resistance', 171.
11. *Hampshire Telegraph*, 12 May 1823.
12. Sheridan, *Doctors and Slaves*, 227.
13. Ibid.
14. Long, *The History of Jamaica*, quoted in Bush, 126.
15. Higman, *Slave Populations of the British Caribbean*, 308.
16. Ibid.
17. Some historians have concluded that the harsh demands of sugar production were a 'paramount cause' of the slaves' continuing demographic decline. Others, like Higman, have

blamed marital instability and casual mating patterns. Orlando Patterson has argued that female promiscuity may have been partly to blame. However unintentionally, such views seem to echo of the arguments put forward by the planters themselves.

18. Dunn, 'A Tale of Two Plantations'.

19. Sheridan, *Doctors and Slaves*, 240.

20. Letters from Webb to Barham (1810–1812).

21. Letters from John Shand to George Pennant (1814), ibid.

22. Lewis, *Journal of a West India Proprietor*, 381.

23. Prince, *The History of Mary Prince*.

24. Leonard Barratt, 'Portrait of a Jamaican Healer: African Medicinal Lore in the Caribbean', *Caribbean Quarterly*, 9, 3, 1973, 16.

25. Long, *The History of Jamaica*, 381.

26. Dr Robert Thomas's *Evidence to the House of Commons Select Committee* (1790) in B.S.P., 252

27. Evidence of Dr Michael Clare, *House of Lords Report* (1832), Part I, 274–5.

28. J. M. Allain, 'Infanticide as Slave Resistance: Evidence from Barbados, Jamaica, and Saint-Domingue', *Inquiries*, 6, 4, 2014.

29. Stedman, *Narrative of a Five-Year Expedition, Volume 2*, 368.

30. Evidence of John Baillie, *House of Lords Report* (1832), 51.

31. See Michael P. Johnson, 'Smothered Slave Infants: Were Slave Mothers at Fault?', *Journal of Southern History*, 47, 4, 493–520, in which he explores why enslaved African American mothers were nine times more likely than white women to smother their children.

32. Sheridan, *Doctors and Slaves*, 339.

33. Lewis, *Journal of a West India Proprietor*, 82.

Chapter 7

1. For more on this argument, see Edward Kamau Braithwaite, *The Folk Culture of the Slaves of Jamaica* (London: New Beacon, 1974).

2. Bryan Edwards, *History, Civil and Commercial, of the British Colonies in the West Indies* (London: Elder & Co., 1801).

3. Craton, 'Death, Disease and Medicine on the Jamaican Slave Plantations', 57.

4. For a fuller discussion of Nanny, see Craton, 'Death, Disease and Medicine on the Jamaican Slave Plantations', 84–91; Alan Tuelon's article 'Nanny – Maroon Chieftess' in *Caribbean Quarterly*, 19, 1973, 20–7.

5. Joseph J. Williams, *The Maroons of Jamaica* (Anthropological Series of the Boston College Graduate School, 1938), 388.

6. *Calendar of State Papers – America & the West Indies* (1735) quoted in Tuelon, 'Nanny – Maroon Chieftess', 22.

7. Philip Thicknesse, *Memoirs and Anecdotes* (London, 1788), 123.

8. Tuelon, 'Nanny – Maroon Chieftess', 23.

9. Ibid., 25.

10. For a more detailed account of the way black women were viewed by contemporary European men, see Barbara Bush's arguments in *Slave Women in Caribbean Society*, 11–22; and L. M. Mair, 'The Arrival of the African Women', *Jamaica Journal*, 9, 2&3, 3.

11. Thicknesse, quoted in R. C. Dallas, *History of the Maroons – From their Origin to the Establishment of their Chief Tribe in Sierra Leone, Volume I* (London, 1803), 73.

12. Dallas, *History of the Maroons*, 88, 108.

13. Ibid., 110.

14. Ibid., 50.

15. Interview with Vivian Crawford O.D., 'Maroon is not a Race, it's a Description', *Jamaica Global*, 4 February 2019, jamaicaglobalonline.com.

16. See Isert, *Letters on West Africa and the Slave Trade*, 178–82.

17. Ibid., 188.

18. Beckford, *A Descriptive Account, Vol. 2*, 175.

19. Lewis, *Journal of a West India Proprietor*, 90.

20. John Stewart, *A View of the Past and Present State of the Island of Jamaica (with Remarks on the Moral and Physical Condition of Slaves and the Abolition of Slavery in the Colonies)* (London: Oliver & Boyd, 1832).

21. Beckford, *A Descriptive Account, Vol. 2*, 324.

22. Stedman, *Narrative of a Five-Year Expedition, Volume 2*.

23. Mary Seacole, *The Wonderful Adventures of Mary Seacole in Many Lands* (New York: Penguin Classics, 2005).

24. See L. M. Mair, 'The Arrival of the African Women', 53.

25. E. K. Braithwaite, *The Folk Culture of the Slaves of Jamaica*, 13.

26. L. M. Mair, 'The Arrival of the African Women', 49.

Afterword

1. For more information, see migrantwomennetwork.org.

2. For more information, see borgenproject.org.

Index